Государственн

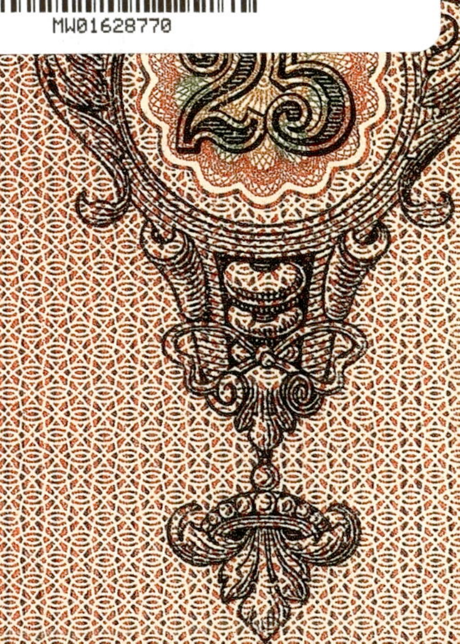

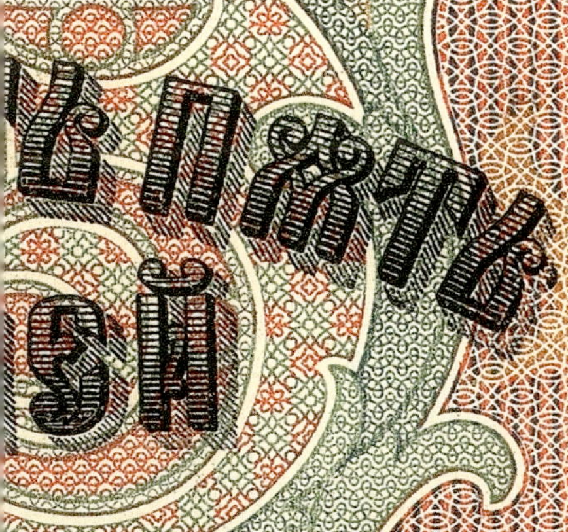

ЙЙ БАНКЪ
ИТНЫЕ БИЛЕТЫ
ОГРАНИЧЕНІЯ СУММЫ
ДЕРЖИТЪ 17, 424 ДОЛЕЙ
ЛОТА).

ЕЛ 443848

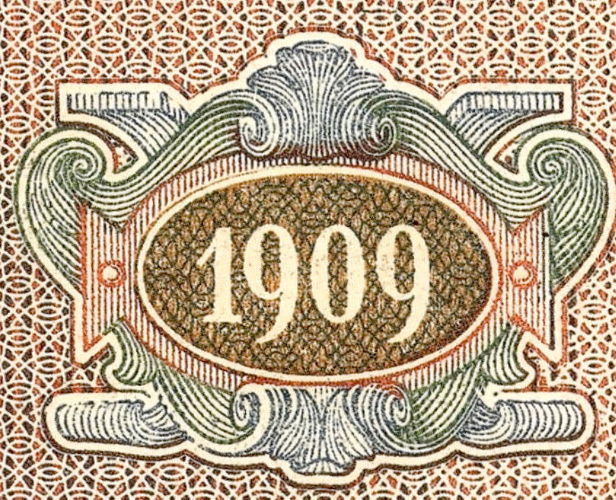

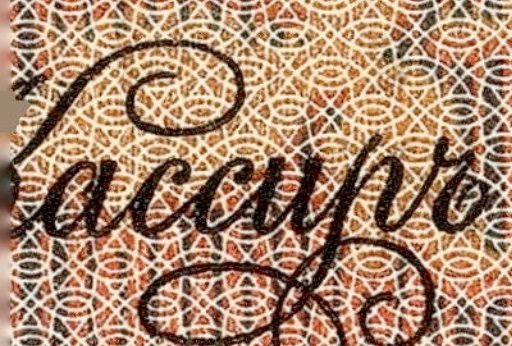

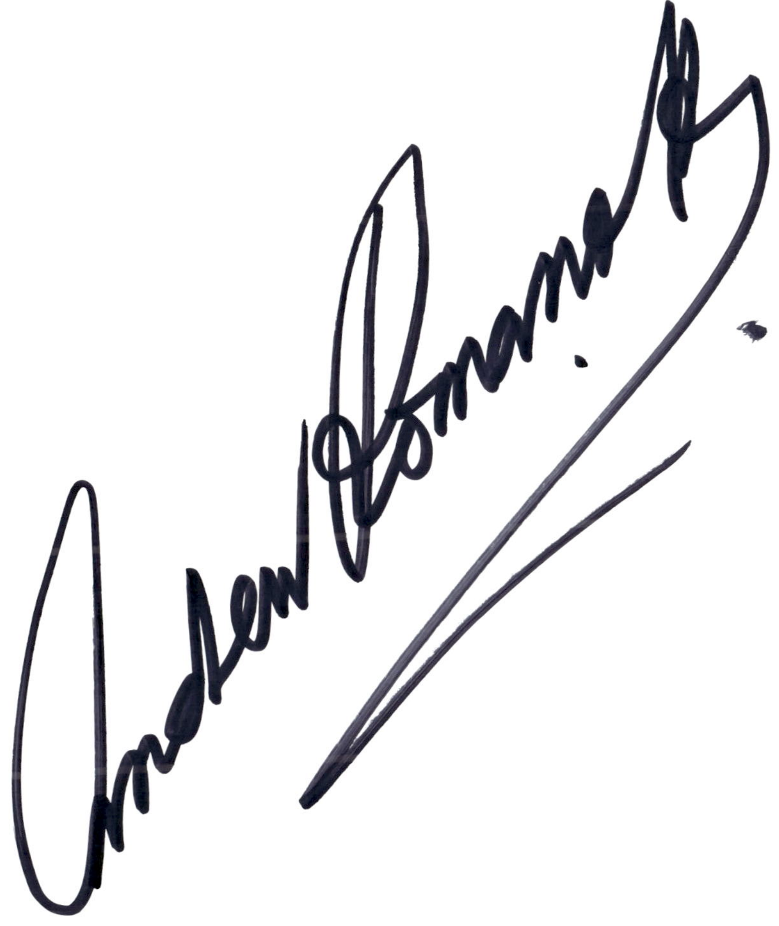

The Boy Who Would Be Tsar

THE ART OF PRINCE ANDREW ROMANOFF

The Boy Who Would Be Tsar: The Art of Prince Andrew Romanoff
Second Edition

ISBN: 0-9777442-2-1

This book accompanies an exhibition of the artwork of Andrew Romanoff organized by Griff Williams and presented by Gallery 16, San Francisco, January 12-February 23, 2007.

Editor: Christina Amini.
Writers: Rachel Hutton, Tim Gihring, and Nancy Pick.
Book Design: Griff Williams and Urban Digital Color, San Francisco.
Photographs contained in this book are from the personal archive of Prince Andrew Romanoff.

Andrew would like to offer special thanks to Mark Sloan for his encouragement on this project.

R LONDON, S.W. 32
No 2157

LONDON OFFICIAL PAID
21 DEC 37

REGISTERED
21 DEC 37
BUCKINGHAM PALACE, S.W.1

To

Prince Andrew of Russia

Wilderness House

Hampton Court Palace

Middlesex

GRI
VI

E. R.

An Introduction to Prince Andrew Romanoff

Prince Andrew Romanoff might have become Russia's tsar, had fate, in the form of the Bolshevik Revolution, not intervened. Andrew is the grandnephew of Russia's last tsar, Nicholas II, who was murdered along with his family in 1918. Andrew grew up not in Russia but in England, where his family found refuge from the murderous schemes of the Bolsheviks.

As the first cousin of Tsar Nicholas, the English King George V wanted to aid his family. He sent a ship called the H.M.S. Marlborough to rescue Nicholas II's sister, the Grand Duchess Xenia, who was Andrew's grandmother. The king invited Xenia and her family to live in a 23-room "cottage" on the grounds of Windsor Castle.

Andrew was born on January 21, 1923, in London and spent most of his childhood inside the castle gates. The Windsor grounds made for a fantastic playground, with vast lawns, curving paths along the River Thames, fishponds, greenhouses full of exotic plants, and polo fields.

At home, Andrew always spoke Russian, and was expected to behave, well, like a prince. His mother made him practice walking with a stick under his arms so that he would stand up straight, like royalty. Andrew's grandmother never stopped believing that someday the Romanoffs would return to Russian and rule the country once more, as they had since 1613.

Instead, Andrew enlisted with the British Navy and served in World War II. After the war ended, Andrew worked as a farmer outside London in Kent before moving to the United States to join his uncle and aunt in California. In Palo Alto, California, he successfully tried his hand at many different ventures: the import-export business, acting as a timekeeper for a shipping company, carpentry, and art.

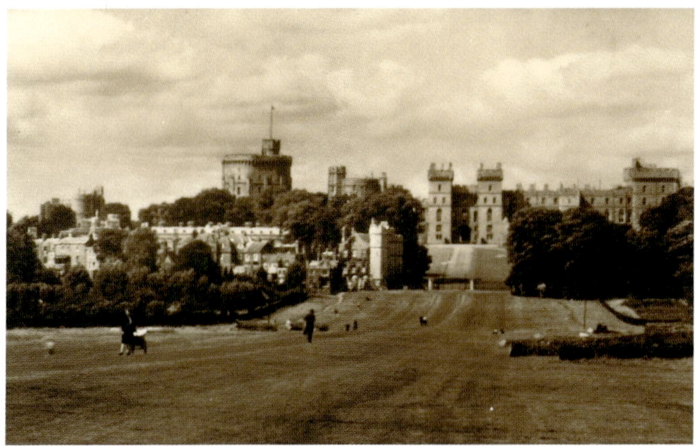

Windsor Castle from Longwalk, 1935.

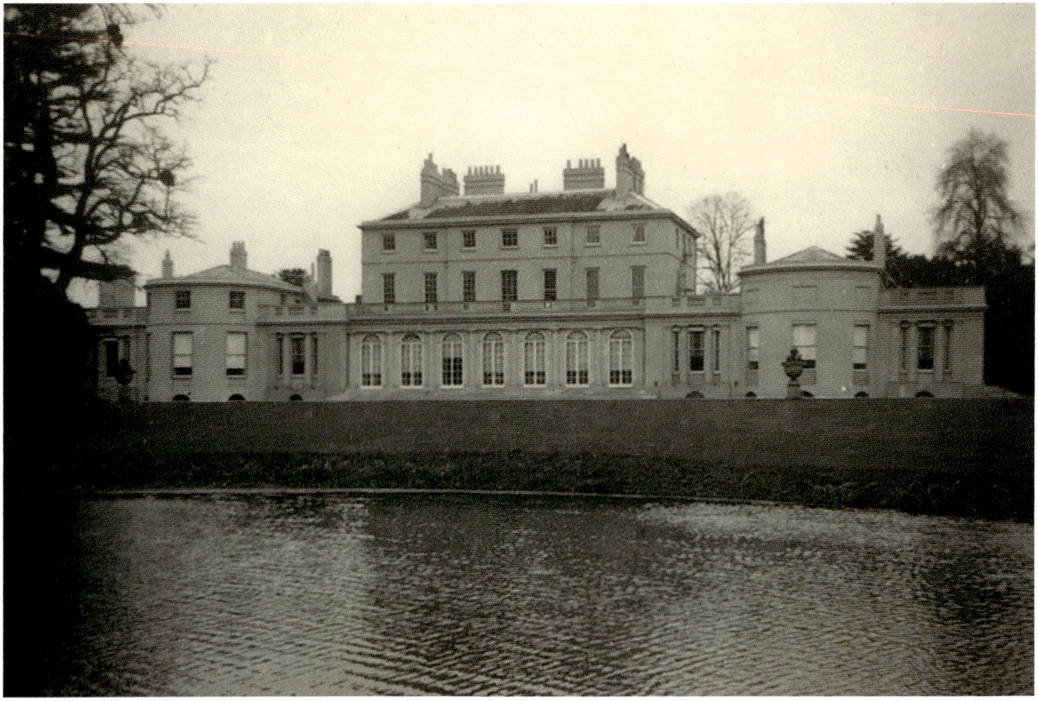

Frogmore House, 1935.

Today, Andrew lives outside of San Francisco in Inverness with his wife, artist Inez Storer. On his preferred medium of Shrinky Dinks (plastic sheets that shrink by two-thirds when cooked in an oven), Andrew draws and paints, shrinks the inimitable scenes, then mounts them on painted panels. Andrew's unique, utterly original artwork is firmly rooted in the traditions of Folk Art. There is a refreshingly earnest humor in the choice of material and in the witty execution of Andrew's deceptively simple renderings. His work typically depicts personal memories, impressions of American news, culture, and scenes of domestic life. In this book, presented at their original size, Andrew's modern version of Russian miniatures chronicle a most unusual, almost magical, childhood.

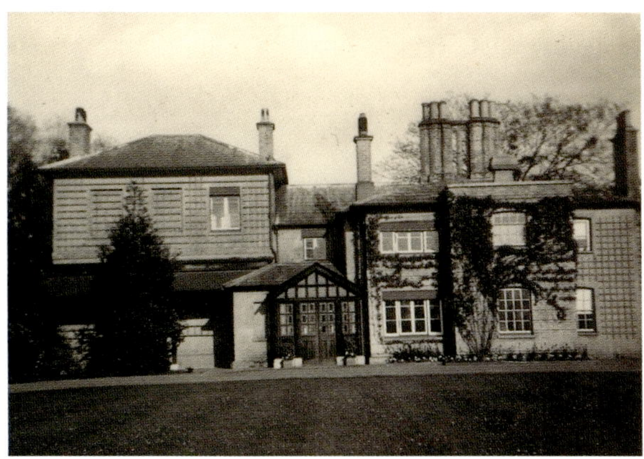

Frogmore Cottage on the grounds at Windsor. King George V gave Xenia the "grace and favour" house in 1925. This was the home in which Andrew was raised.

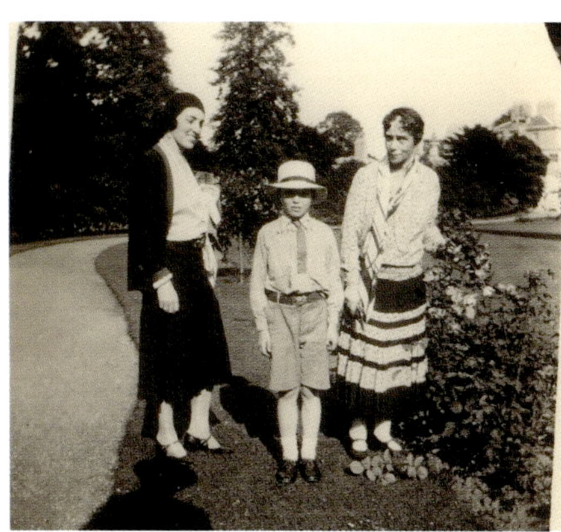

Andrew with his mother (left) and grandmother, Grand Duchess Xenia (right), on the grounds of Windsor, 1928.

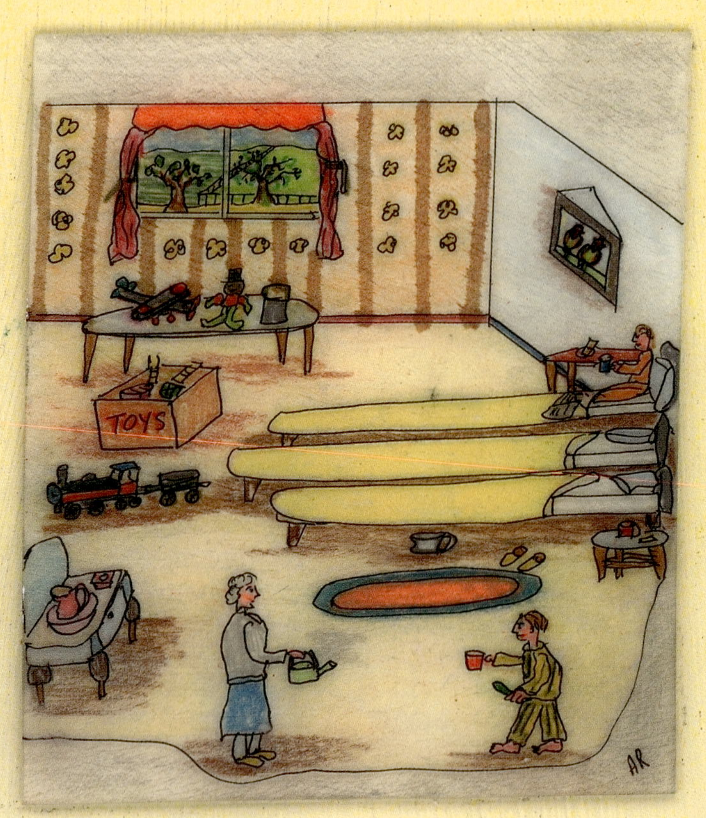

NANNY BROUGHT TEA AND BISCUITS FOR ANDREW IN BED

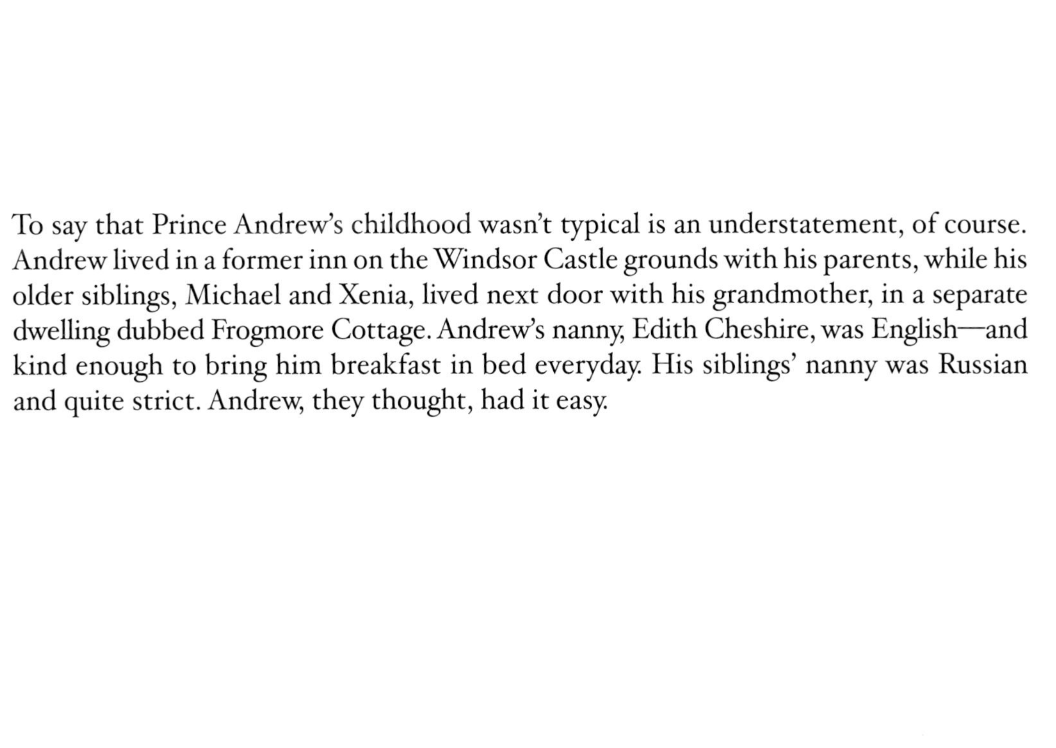

To say that Prince Andrew's childhood wasn't typical is an understatement, of course. Andrew lived in a former inn on the Windsor Castle grounds with his parents, while his older siblings, Michael and Xenia, lived next door with his grandmother, in a separate dwelling dubbed Frogmore Cottage. Andrew's nanny, Edith Cheshire, was English—and kind enough to bring him breakfast in bed everyday. His siblings' nanny was Russian and quite strict. Andrew, they thought, had it easy.

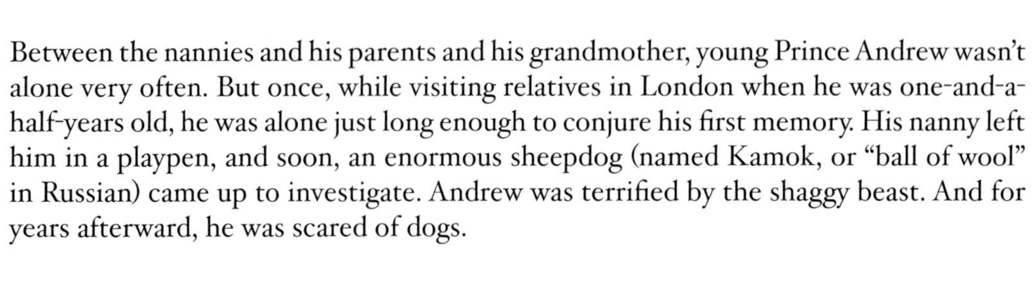

Between the nannies and his parents and his grandmother, young Prince Andrew wasn't alone very often. But once, while visiting relatives in London when he was one-and-a-half-years old, he was alone just long enough to conjure his first memory. His nanny left him in a playpen, and soon, an enormous sheepdog (named Kamok, or "ball of wool" in Russian) came up to investigate. Andrew was terrified by the shaggy beast. And for years afterward, he was scared of dogs.

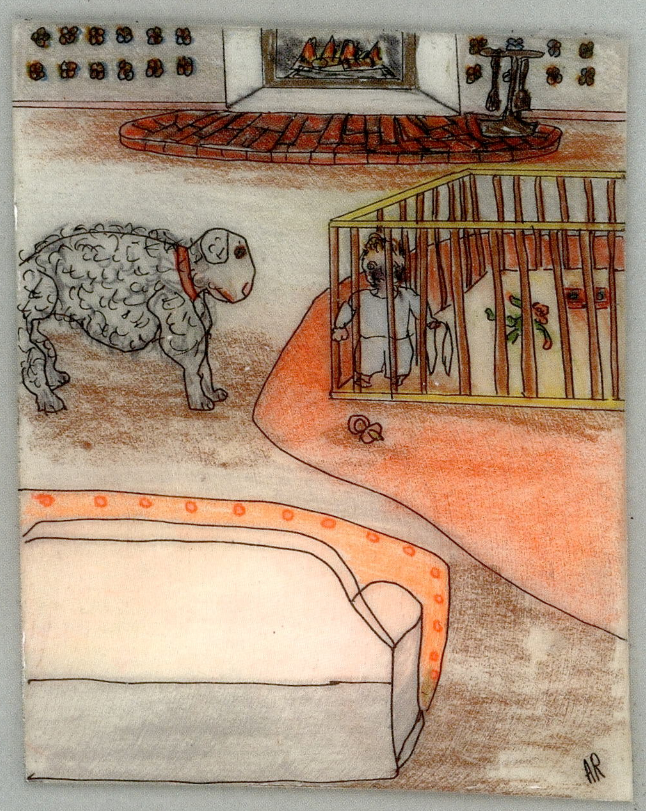

LEFT ALONE WITH DOG
"KAMOK" SCARED ME

Prince Andrew and his family didn't socialize much with the British royal family, despite living on their castle grounds. But every so often, there were encounters. When Andrew was about six, his grandmother took him to meet Queen Mary at the castle. She patted him on the head and said, "You may call me Auntie Mary." Queen Mary, who died in 1953, was the grandmother of Elizabeth II, the current queen of England. She was tall and always wore a veil, in the fashion of the day. Andrew did indeed call her Auntie Mary, and he called her husband, King George V, Uncle Bertie.

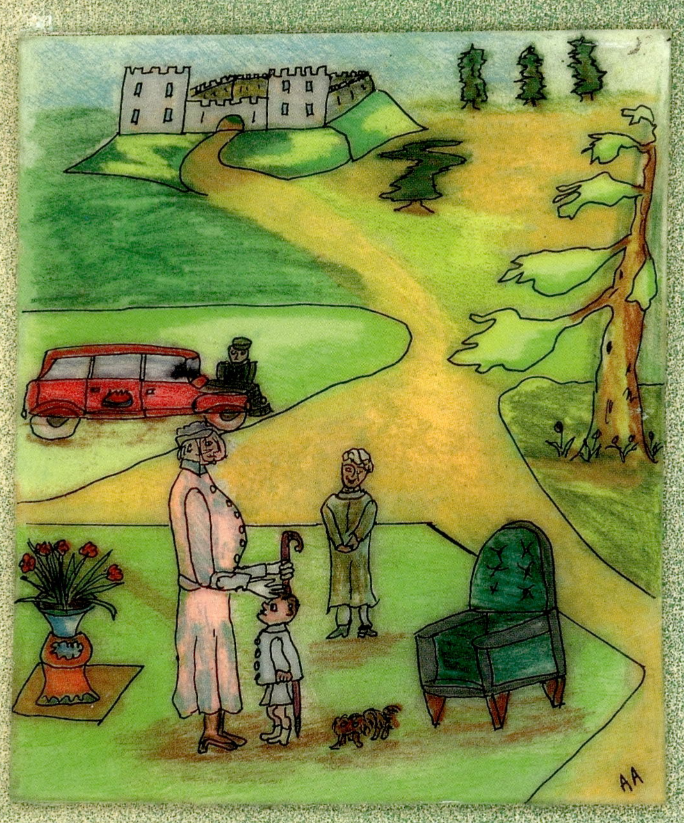

QUEEN MARY SAYS you CAN CALL ME AUNTIE MARY

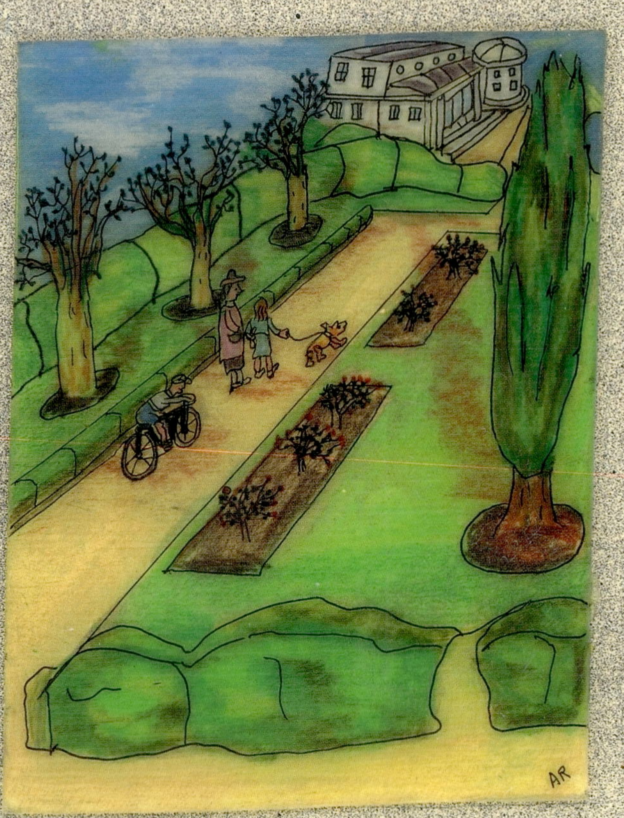

ANDREW BUMPS INTO YOUNG

PRINCESS ELIZABETH.

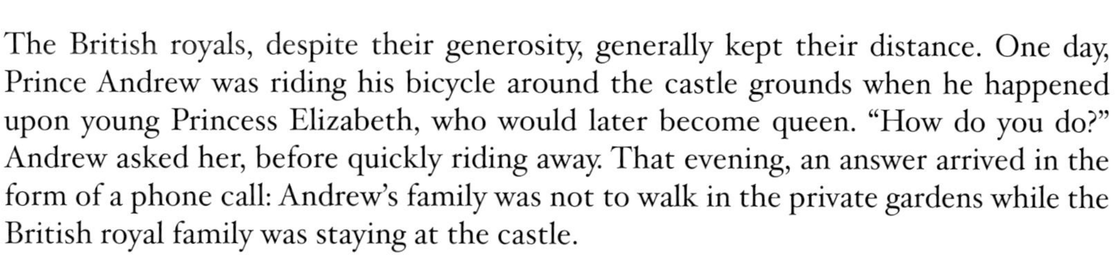

The British royals, despite their generosity, generally kept their distance. One day, Prince Andrew was riding his bicycle around the castle grounds when he happened upon young Princess Elizabeth, who would later become queen. "How do you do?" Andrew asked her, before quickly riding away. That evening, an answer arrived in the form of a phone call: Andrew's family was not to walk in the private gardens while the British royal family was staying at the castle.

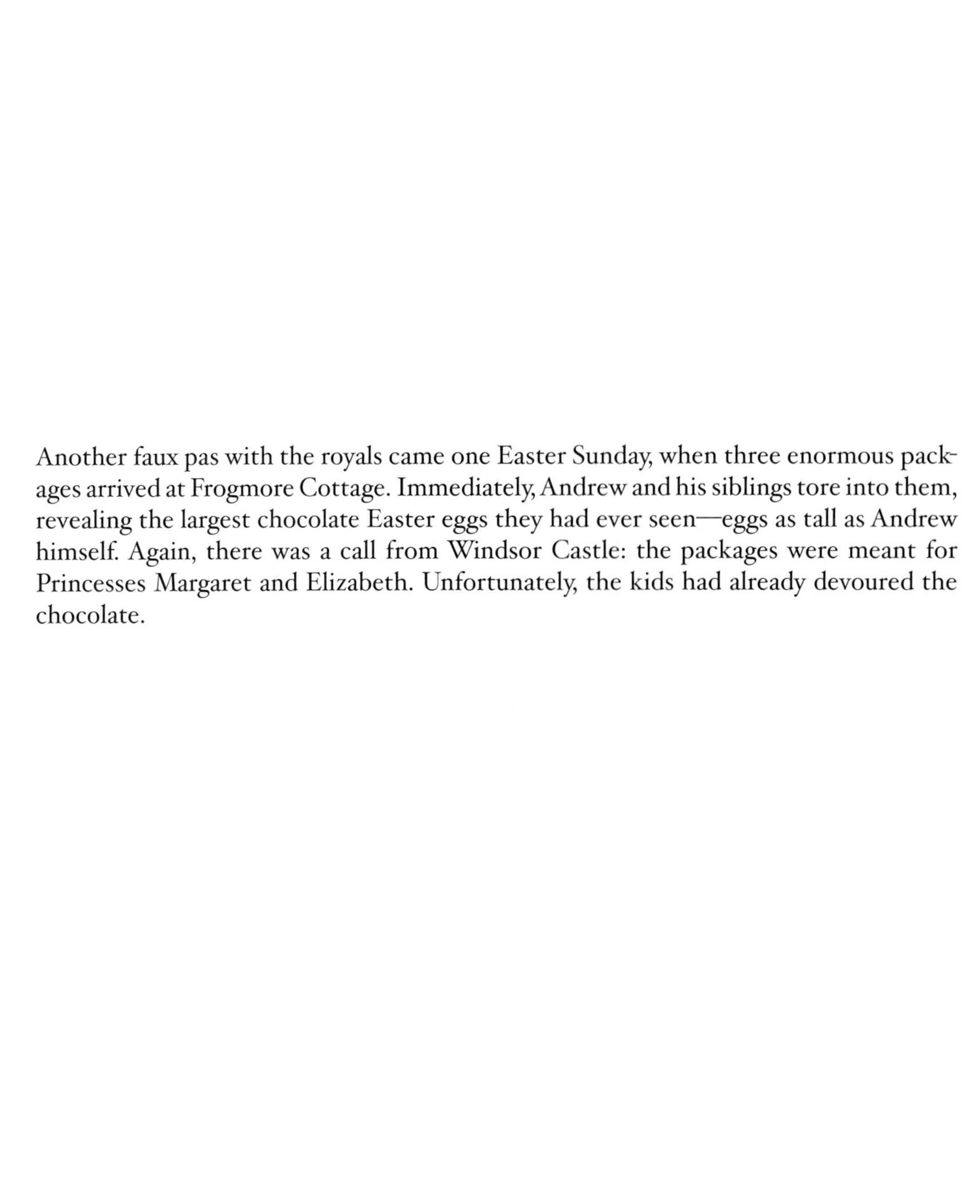

Another faux pas with the royals came one Easter Sunday, when three enormous packages arrived at Frogmore Cottage. Immediately, Andrew and his siblings tore into them, revealing the largest chocolate Easter eggs they had ever seen—eggs as tall as Andrew himself. Again, there was a call from Windsor Castle: the packages were meant for Princesses Margaret and Elizabeth. Unfortunately, the kids had already devoured the chocolate.

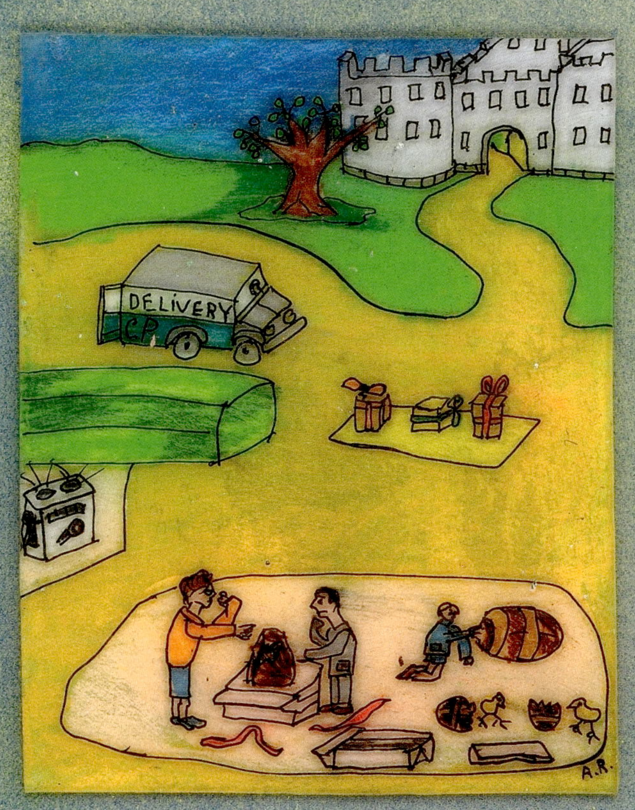

We ate Easter eggs meant for Princess Elizabeth and Margaret

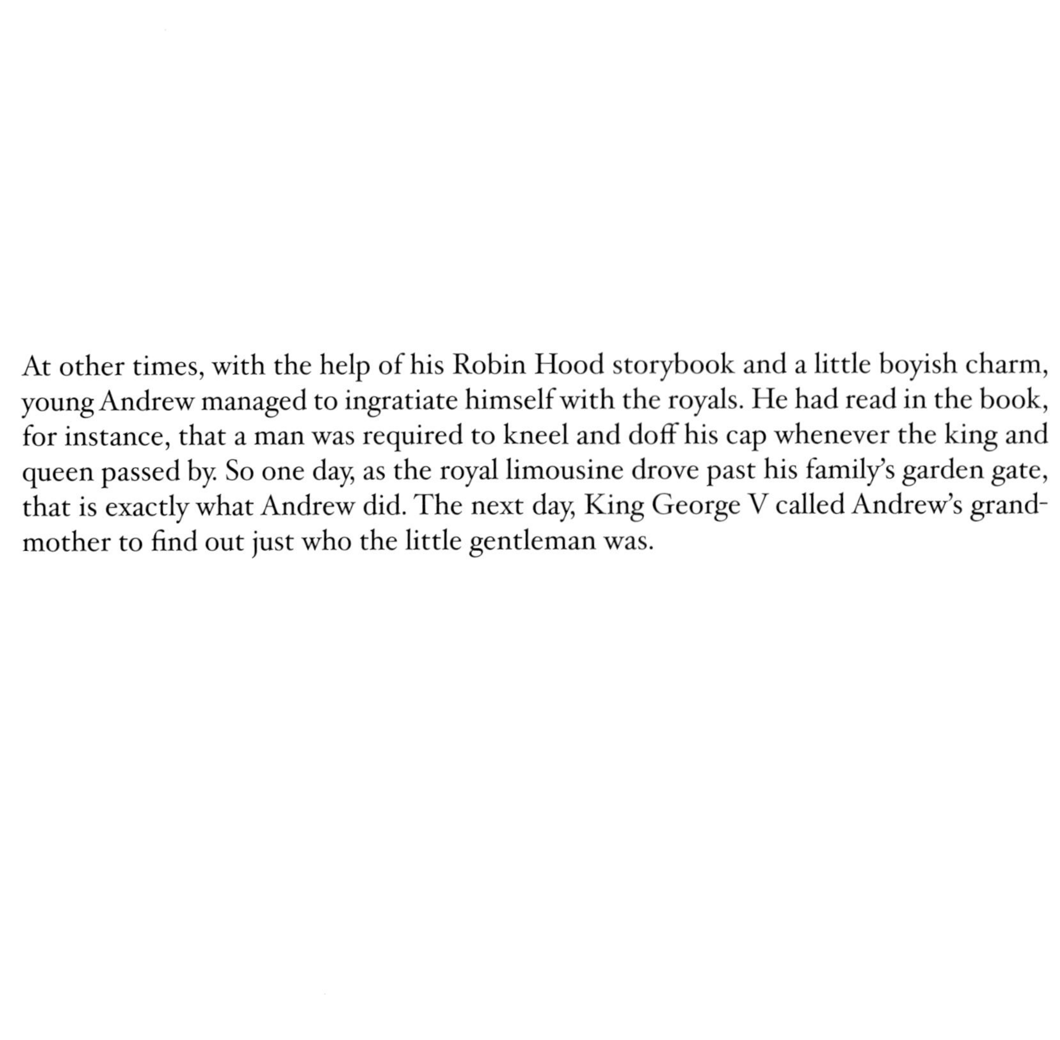

At other times, with the help of his Robin Hood storybook and a little boyish charm, young Andrew managed to ingratiate himself with the royals. He had read in the book, for instance, that a man was required to kneel and doff his cap whenever the king and queen passed by. So one day, as the royal limousine drove past his family's garden gate, that is exactly what Andrew did. The next day, King George V called Andrew's grandmother to find out just who the little gentleman was.

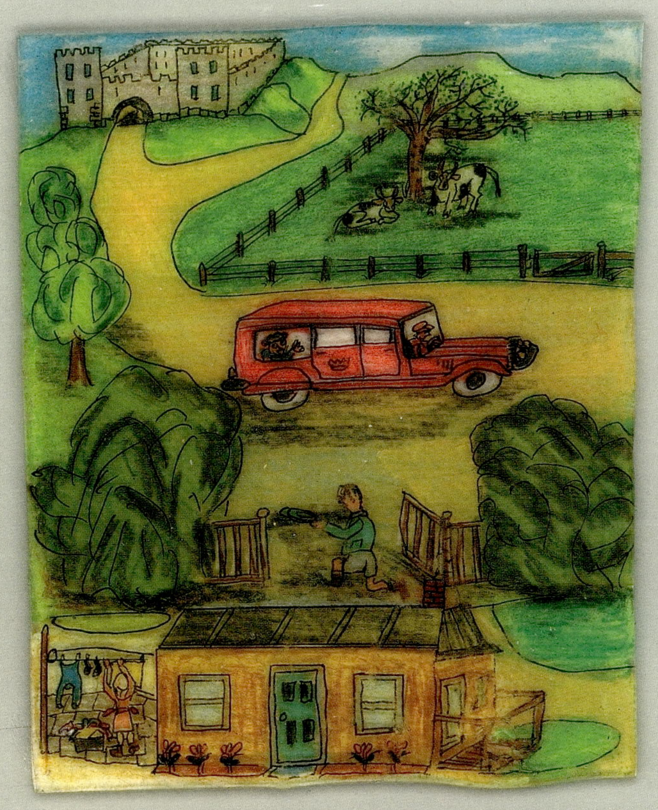

ANDREW KNEELS and TAKES HIS CAP OFF FOR KING

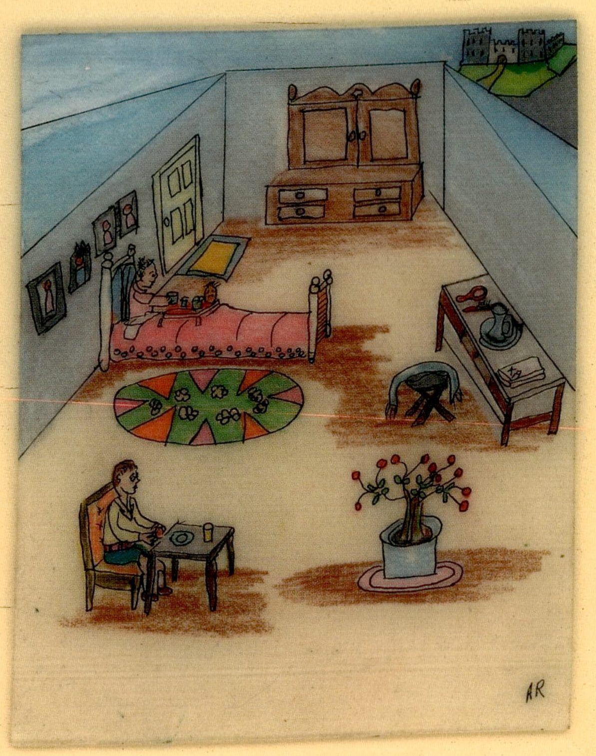

"ANDREW has BREAKFAST with Grandmother"

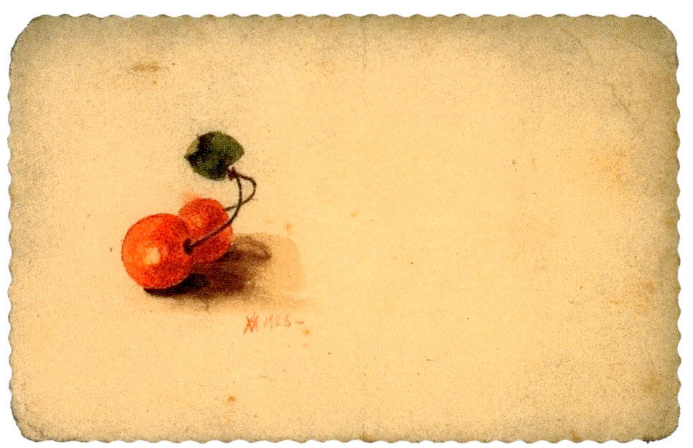

Grand Duchess Xenia, watercolor, 1926.

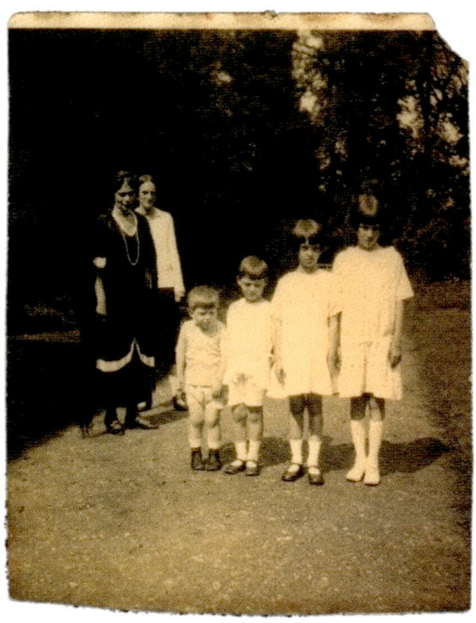

Grandmother Xenia with her daughter Irina and her grandchildren. Andrew is the smallest one in the front.

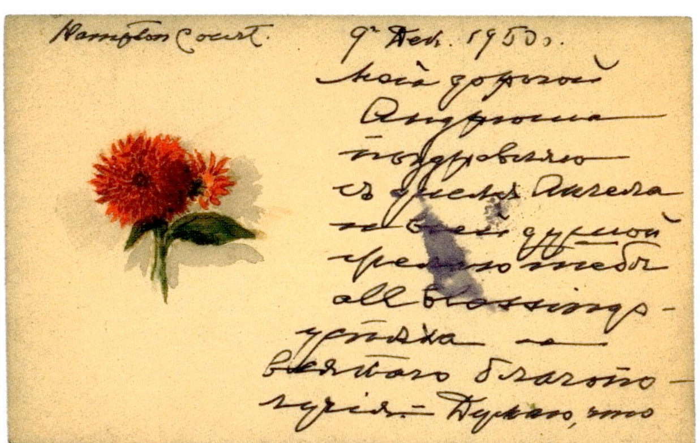

Hampton Court. 9th Feb. 1950.
Мой дорогой
Андрюша
поздравляю
съ днемъ Ангела
и всей душой
желаю тебѣ
all blessings -
успѣха —
всякаго благопо-
лучія. — Думаю, что

Grand Duchess Xenia's watercolor embellished letter written to Andrew, 1950.

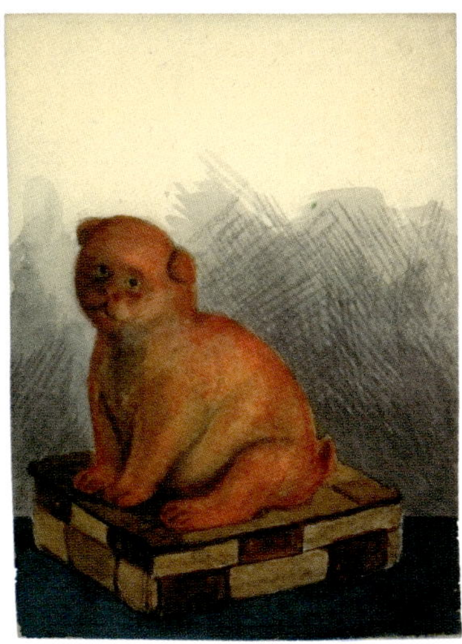

Grand Duchess Xenia, watercolor, 1926.

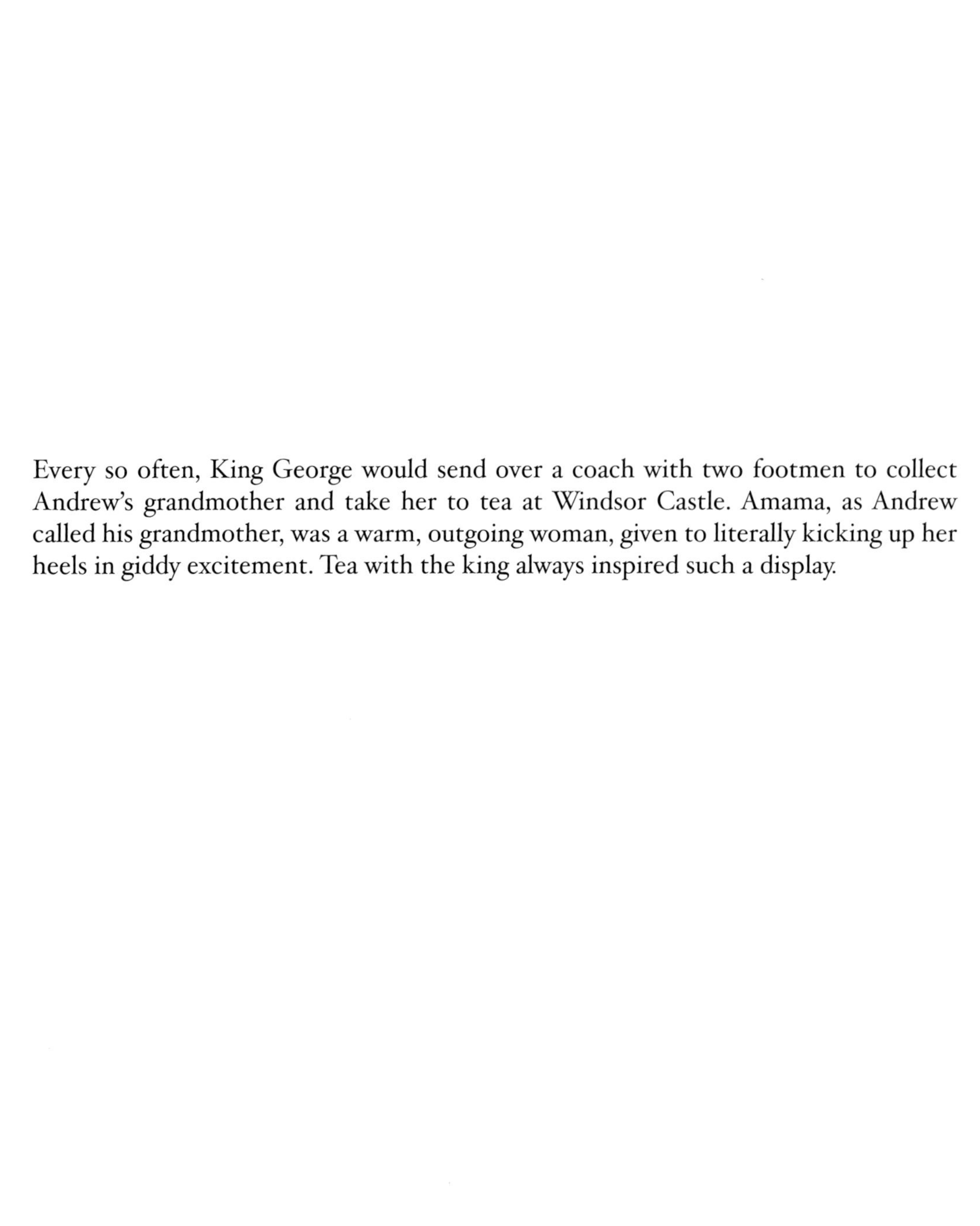

Every so often, King George would send over a coach with two footmen to collect Andrew's grandmother and take her to tea at Windsor Castle. Amama, as Andrew called his grandmother, was a warm, outgoing woman, given to literally kicking up her heels in giddy excitement. Tea with the king always inspired such a display.

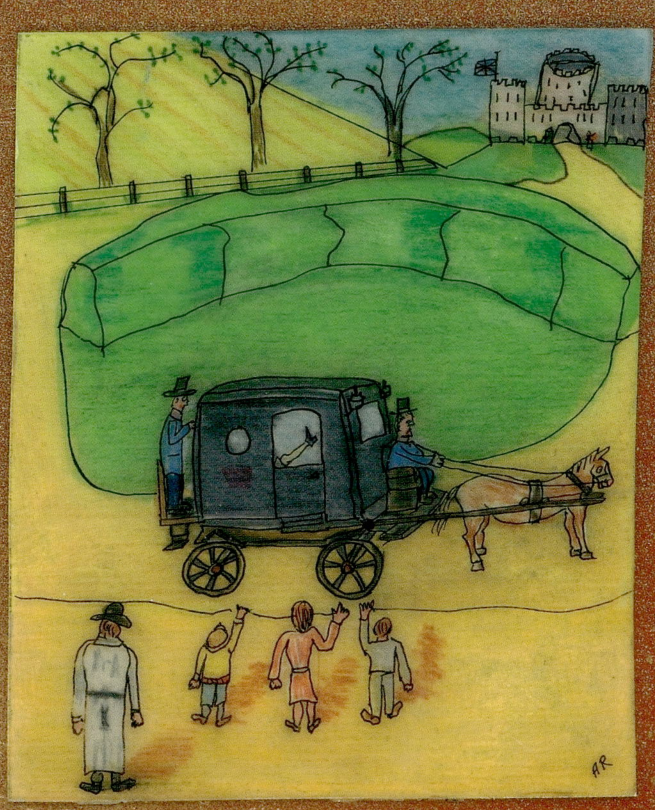

"I am off to Windsor Castle to have tea with King and Queen" as Amama kicks her foot up.

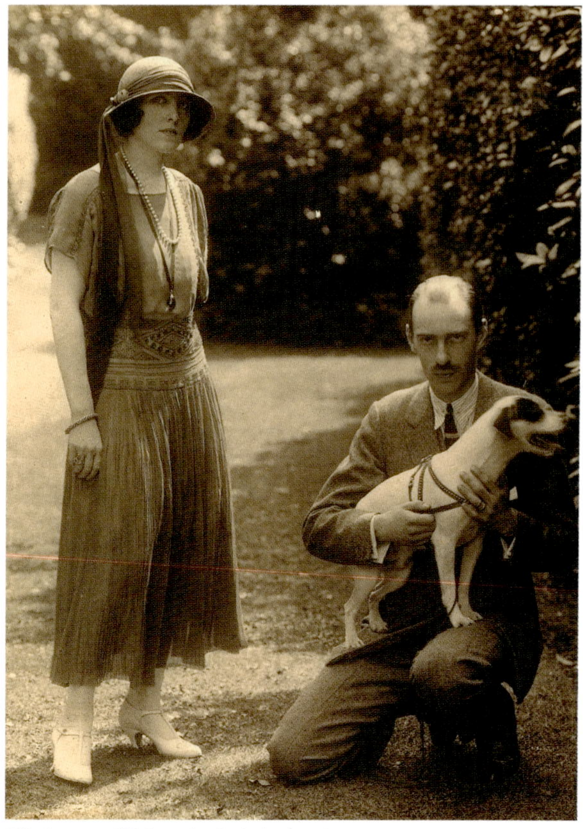

Elisabeta and Prince Andrei, Andrew's parents.

Andrew's mother was Italian on her father's side—her maiden name was Elisabeta Ruffo di Sant' Antimo—and she was known for her wonderful sense of style. She wrote stories for magazines and ran a handbag and scarf design business with Andrew's father.

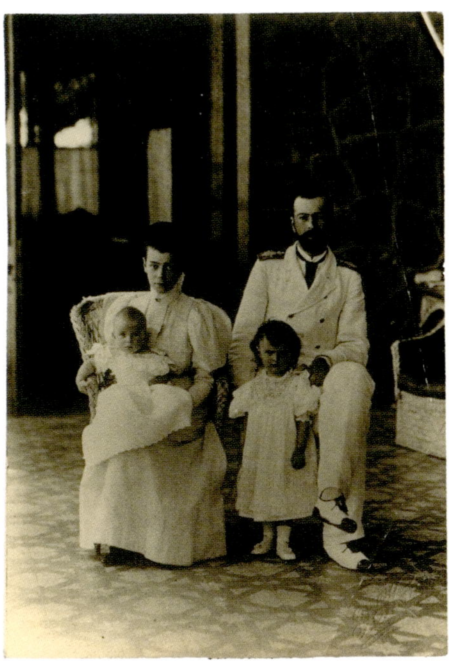

Andrew's grandmother Xenia and grandfather Sandro. Grand Duchess Xenia holds Andrew's father, Prince Andrei, 1897.

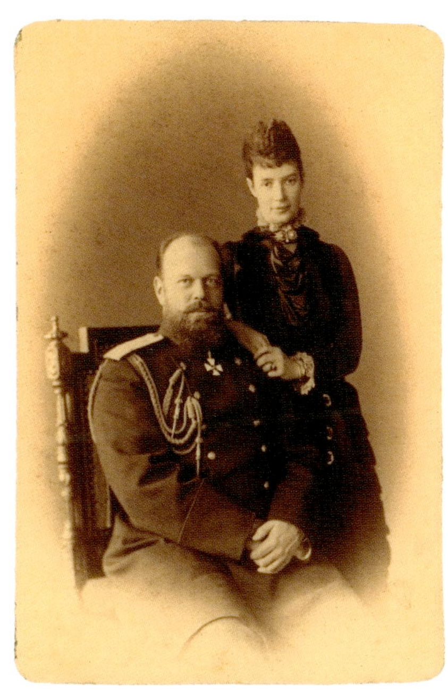

Andrew's great grandfather Tsar Alexander III and grandmother Empress Marie Feodorovna.

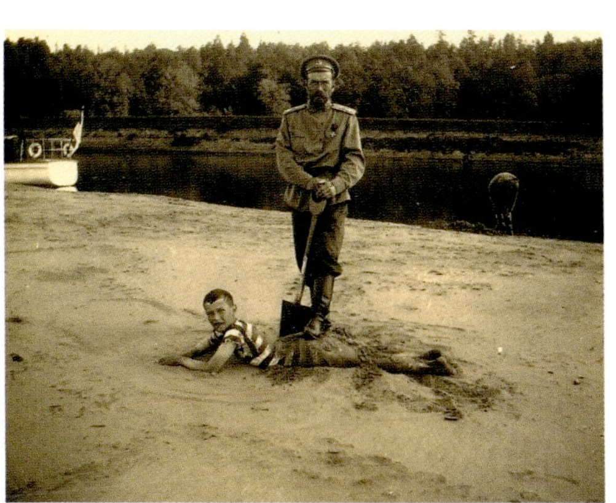

Tsar Nicholas playing on beach with his son.

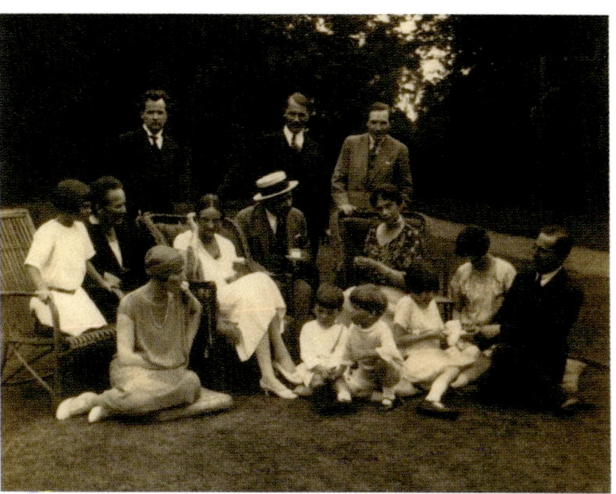

Andrew's family gathering on the grounds at Windsor. Andrew seated in front, 1924.

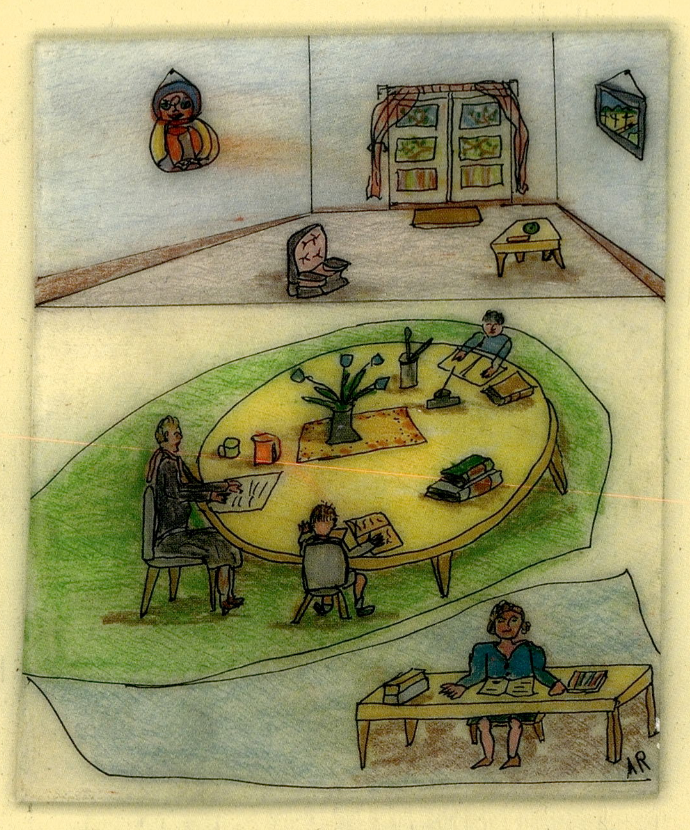
AR

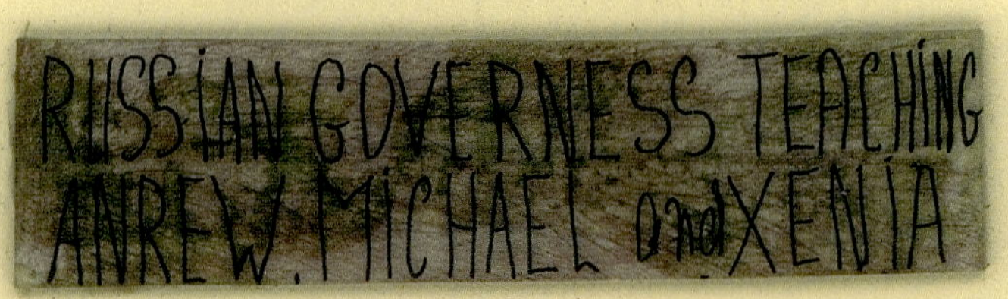
RUSSIAN GOVERNESS TEACHING
ANREW, MICHAEL and XENIA

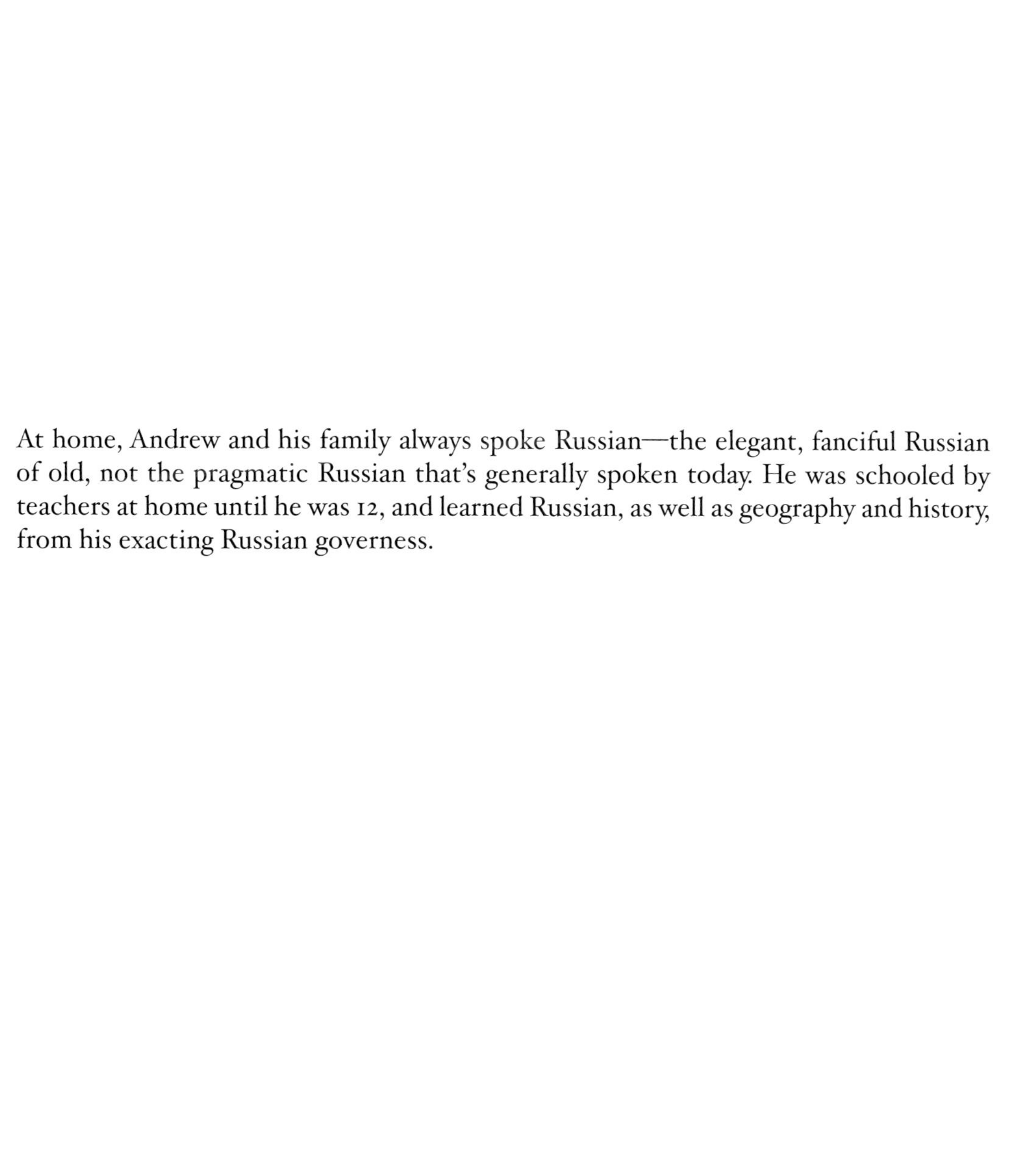

At home, Andrew and his family always spoke Russian—the elegant, fanciful Russian of old, not the pragmatic Russian that's generally spoken today. He was schooled by teachers at home until he was 12, and learned Russian, as well as geography and history, from his exacting Russian governess.

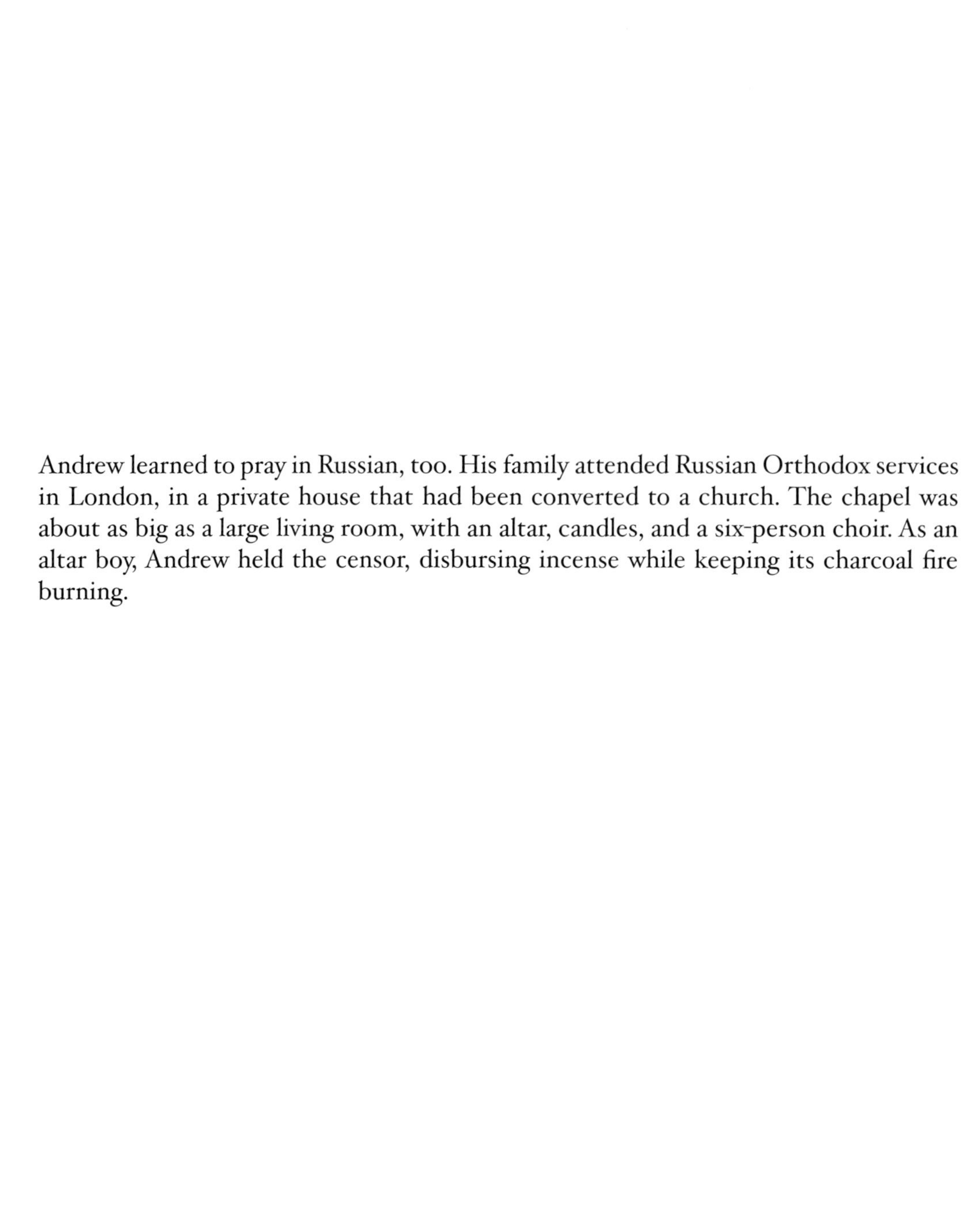

Andrew learned to pray in Russian, too. His family attended Russian Orthodox services in London, in a private house that had been converted to a church. The chapel was about as big as a large living room, with an altar, candles, and a six-person choir. As an altar boy, Andrew held the censor, disbursing incense while keeping its charcoal fire burning.

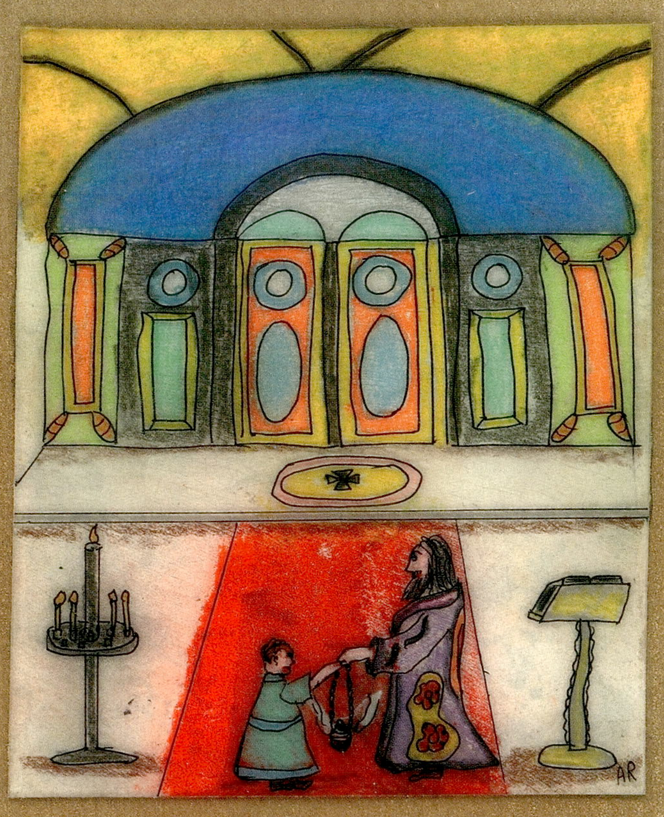

ANDREW AS ALTER BOY

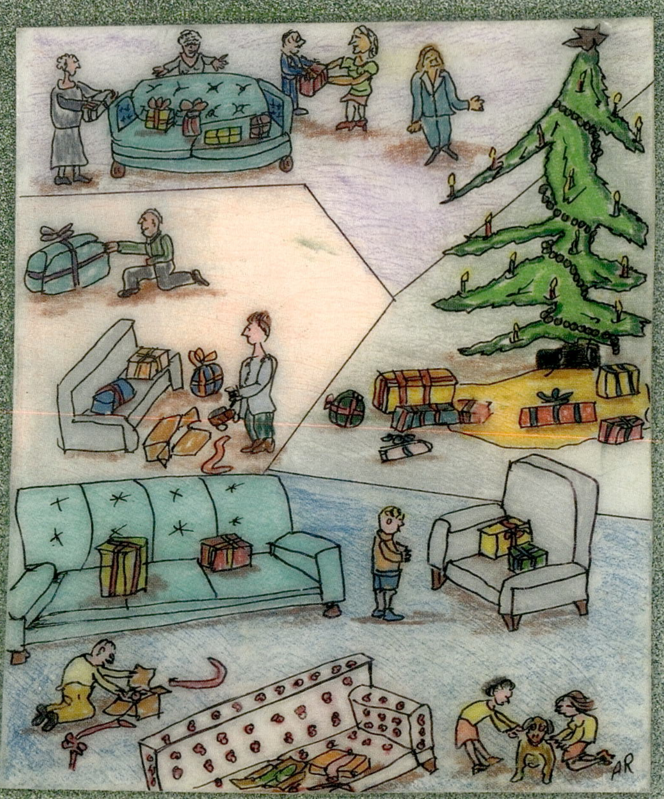

"XMAS PRESENTS WERE PLACED ON COUCHES"

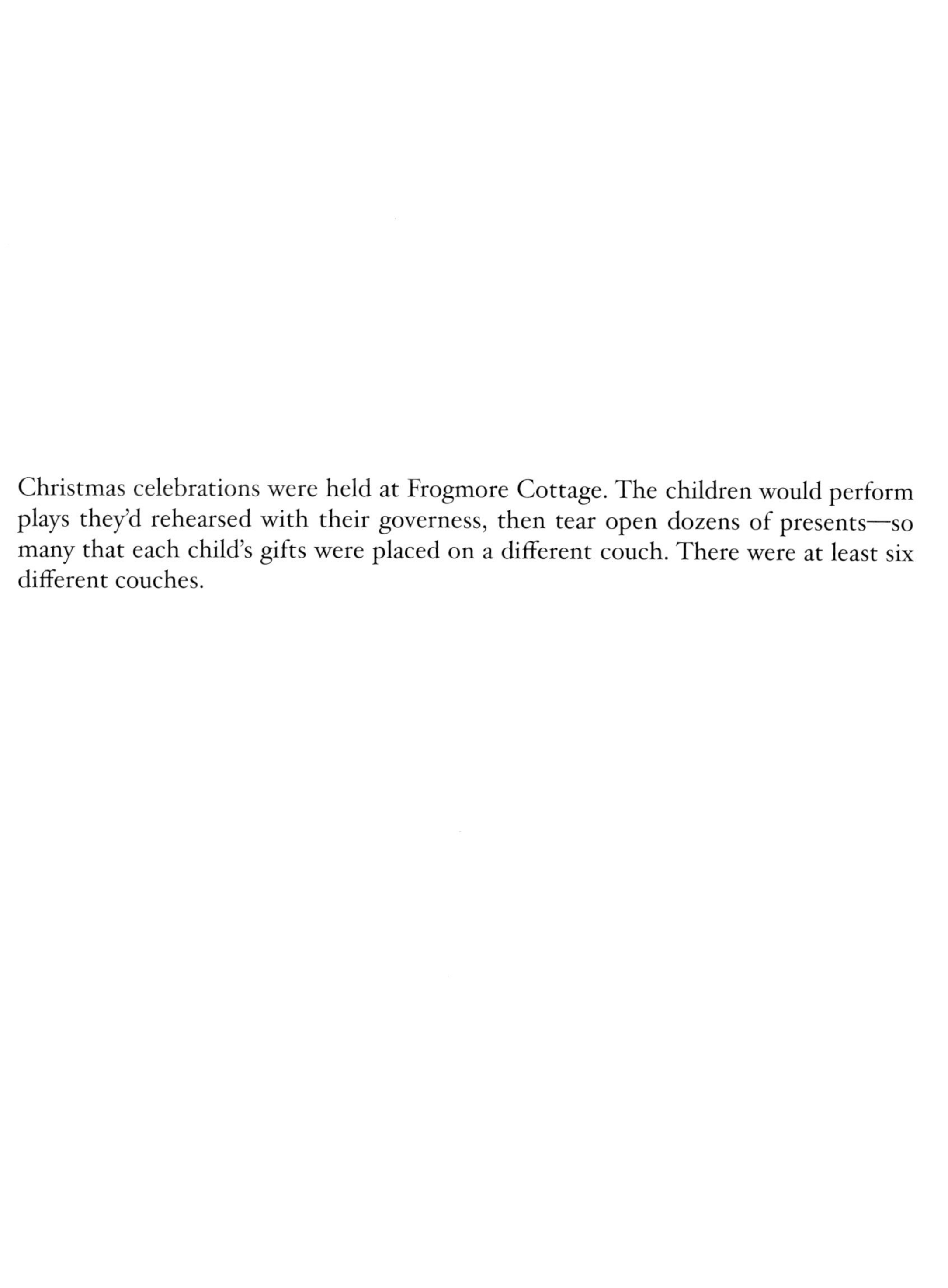

Christmas celebrations were held at Frogmore Cottage. The children would perform plays they'd rehearsed with their governess, then tear open dozens of presents—so many that each child's gifts were placed on a different couch. There were at least six different couches.

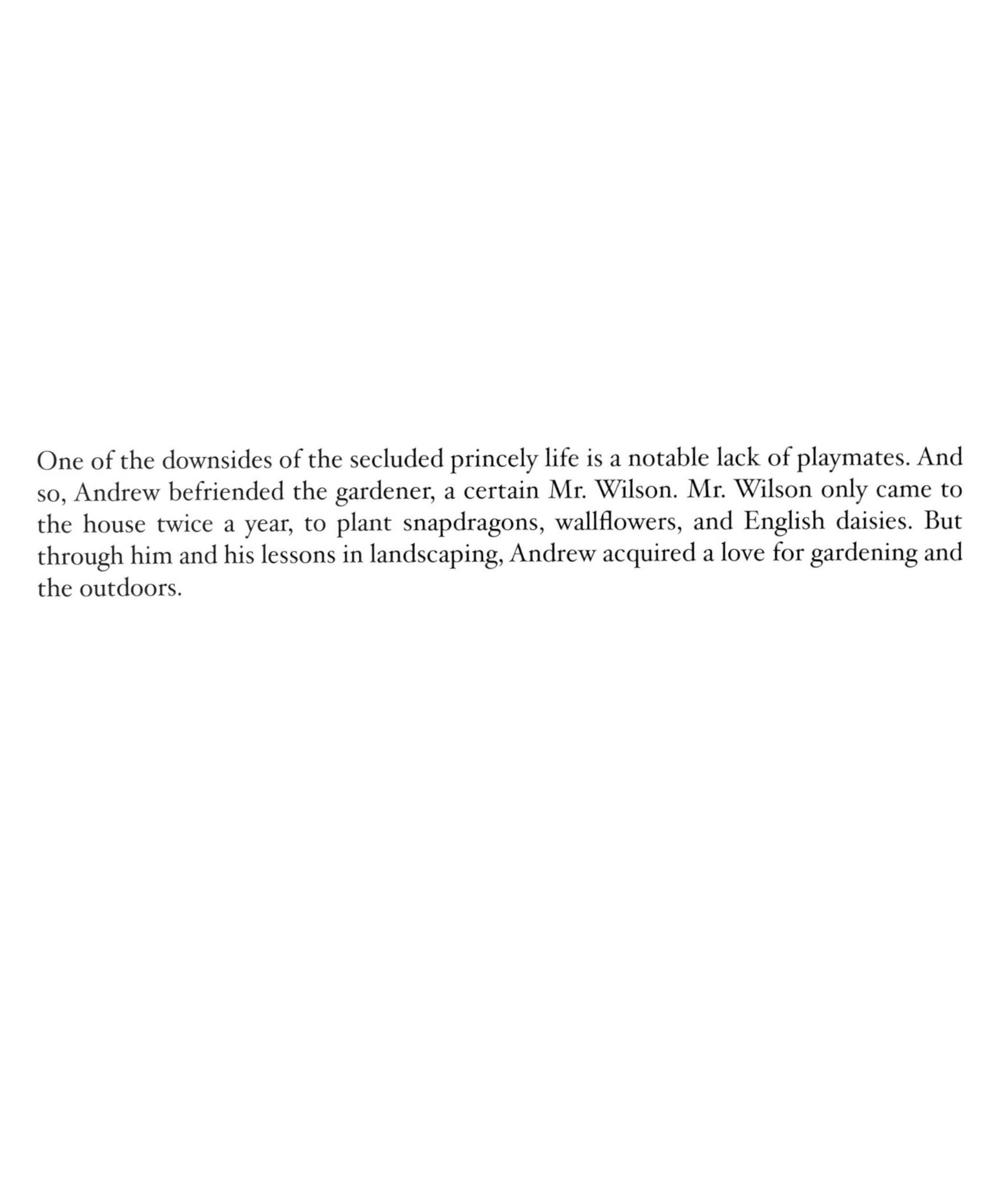

One of the downsides of the secluded princely life is a notable lack of playmates. And so, Andrew befriended the gardener, a certain Mr. Wilson. Mr. Wilson only came to the house twice a year, to plant snapdragons, wallflowers, and English daisies. But through him and his lessons in landscaping, Andrew acquired a love for gardening and the outdoors.

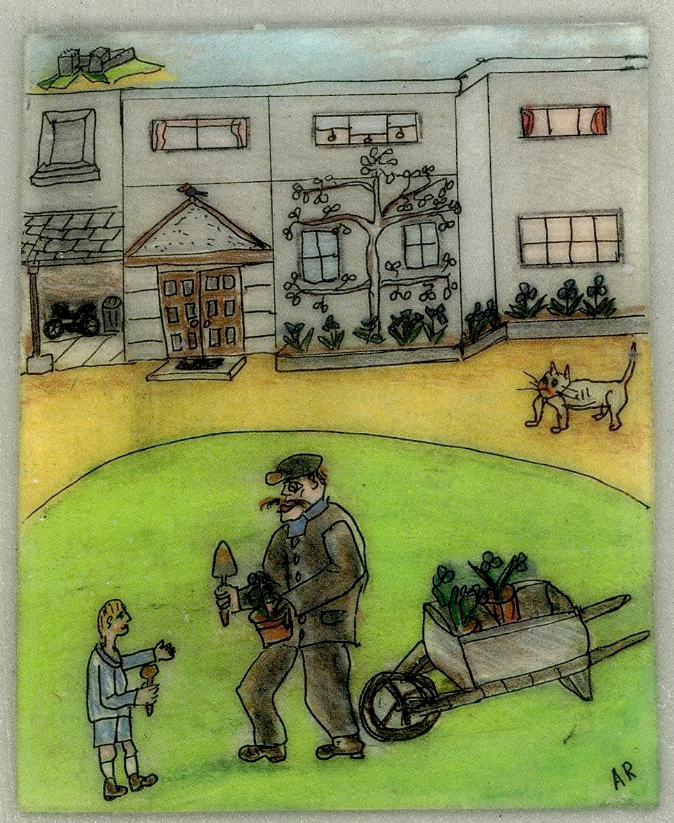

Mr WILSON TEACHES ANDREW HOW TO PLANT FLOWERS

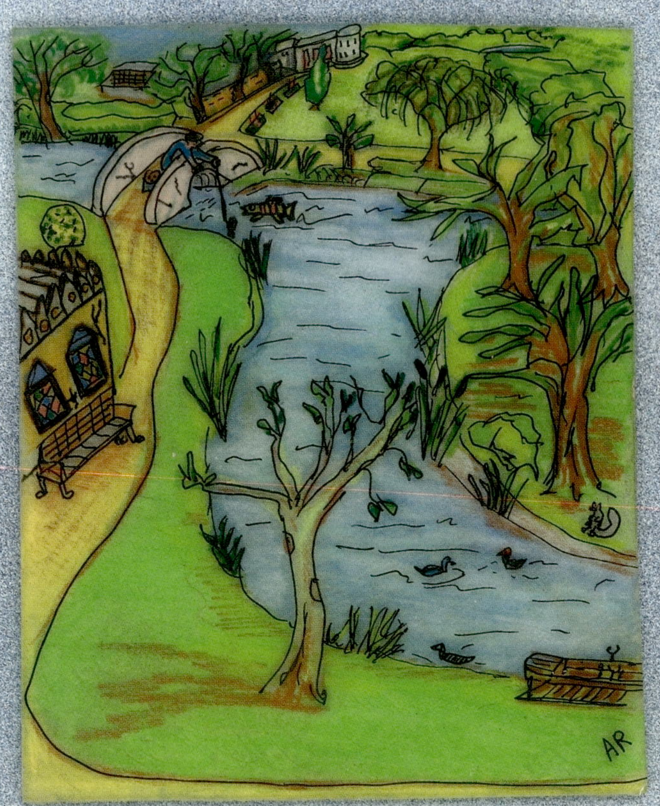

ANDREW CATCHING PERCH
AT SMALL BRIDGE BENT PINS FOR
HOOKS

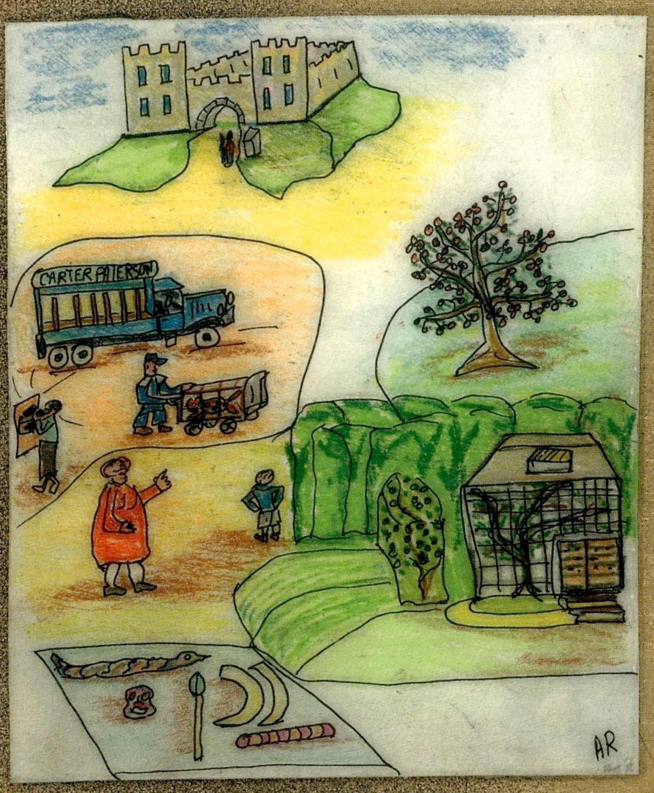

LEOPARD ARRIVES FROM BELGIUM CONGO

The castle grounds were known as Home Park, and Andrew liked nothing better than to roam them, his nanny perpetually by his side. The grounds were so vast that it was easy to be far from home when bad weather blew in, as when Andrew and Miss Cheshire, his nanny, were caught in a storm. They sought shelter under an oak tree, lightning struck, and a large branch crashed to the ground. Luckily, no one was harmed. The two never told Andrew's parents about the close call, as Andrew didn't want his outdoor adventures curtailed and a nanny should know better than to wait out lightning storms under trees.

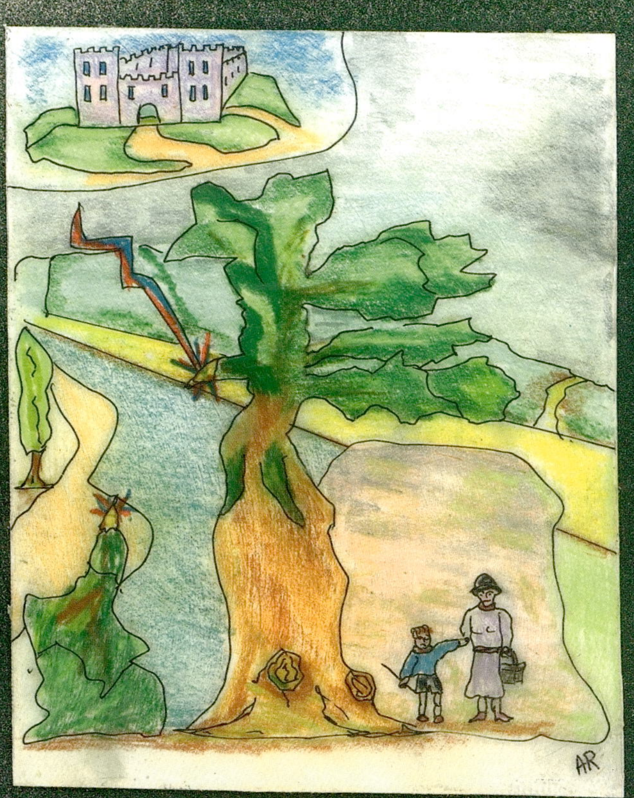

OAK TREE STRUCK by LIGHTNING
NANNY and ANDREW SAFE

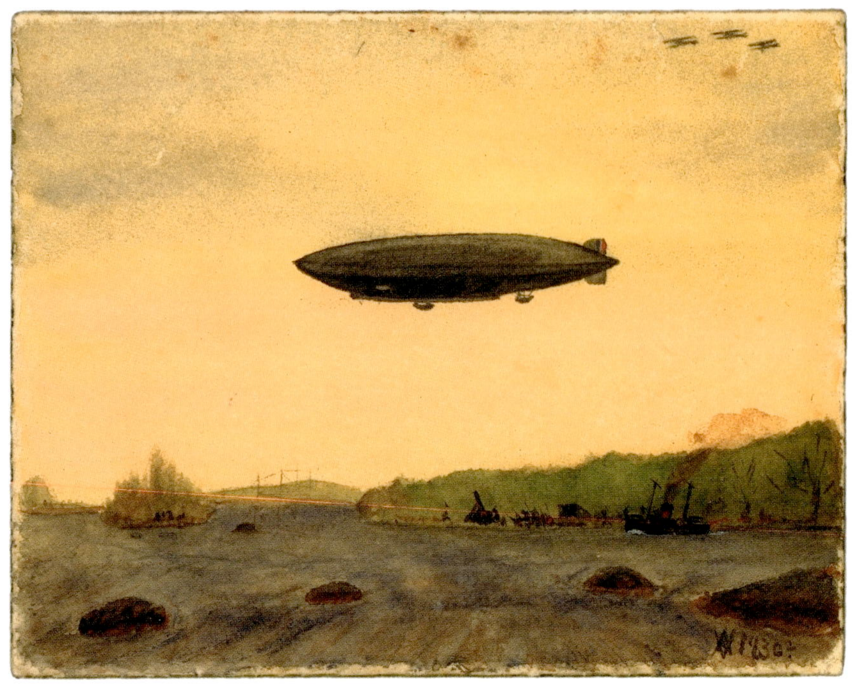

Andrew's father Andrei's watercolor, 1930.

Andrew's father, Prince Andrei Alexandrovich, inspired Andrew's artistic ambitions. Andrei painted oils and watercolors of scenes he recalled from Russia, as well as landscapes of the Windsor Castle gardens, and he showed his work in London galleries. But Andrew's interest took time to bloom. Andrei took him to the top of a hill, set up two easels, and tried to teach him to paint. Andrew attempted a few brushstrokes then abandoned the art lesson to go exploring in the woods.

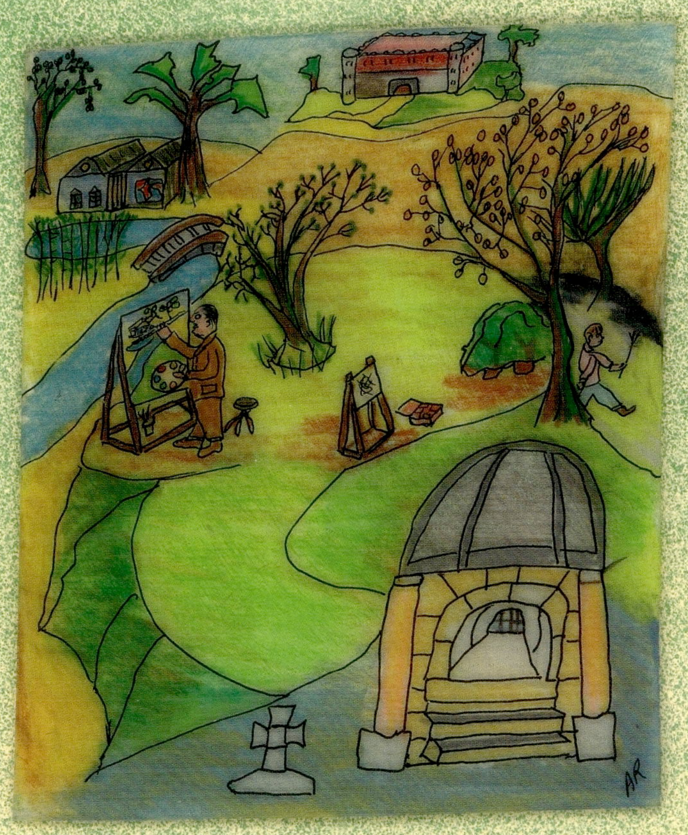

Papa teaching Andrew to paint

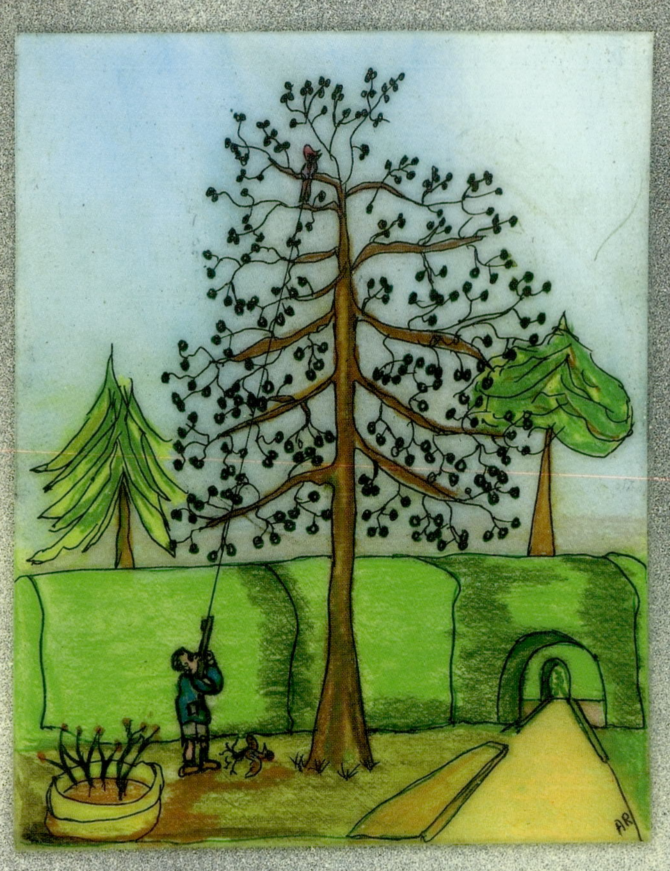

"ANDREW AGED 12 KILLS SINGING BIRD"

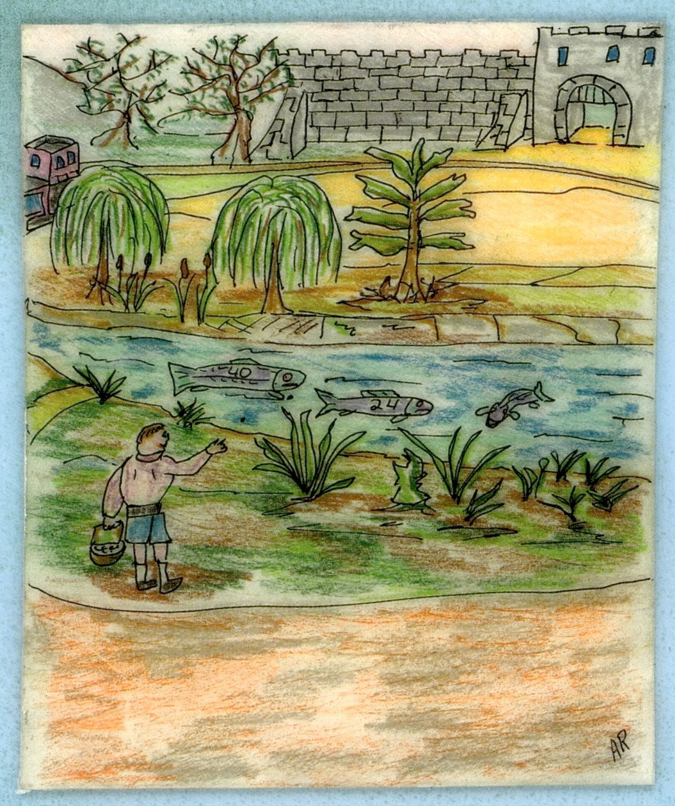

100 YR. OLD CARP WITH NUMBERS RAISED FOR QUEEN VICTORIA

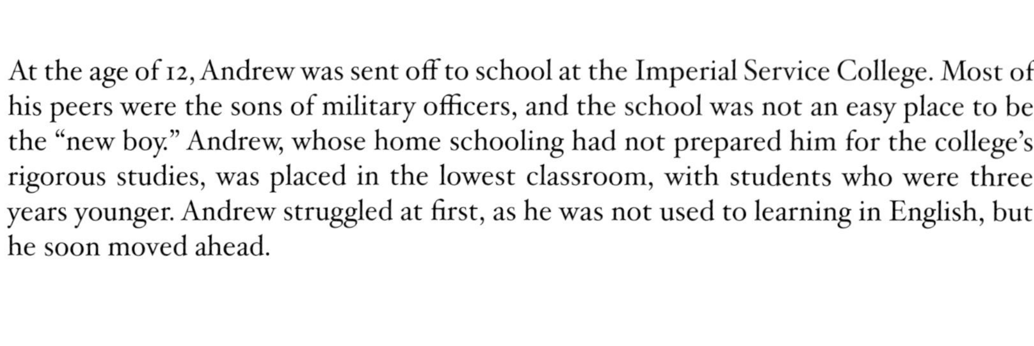

At the age of 12, Andrew was sent off to school at the Imperial Service College. Most of his peers were the sons of military officers, and the school was not an easy place to be the "new boy." Andrew, whose home schooling had not prepared him for the college's rigorous studies, was placed in the lowest classroom, with students who were three years younger. Andrew struggled at first, as he was not used to learning in English, but he soon moved ahead.

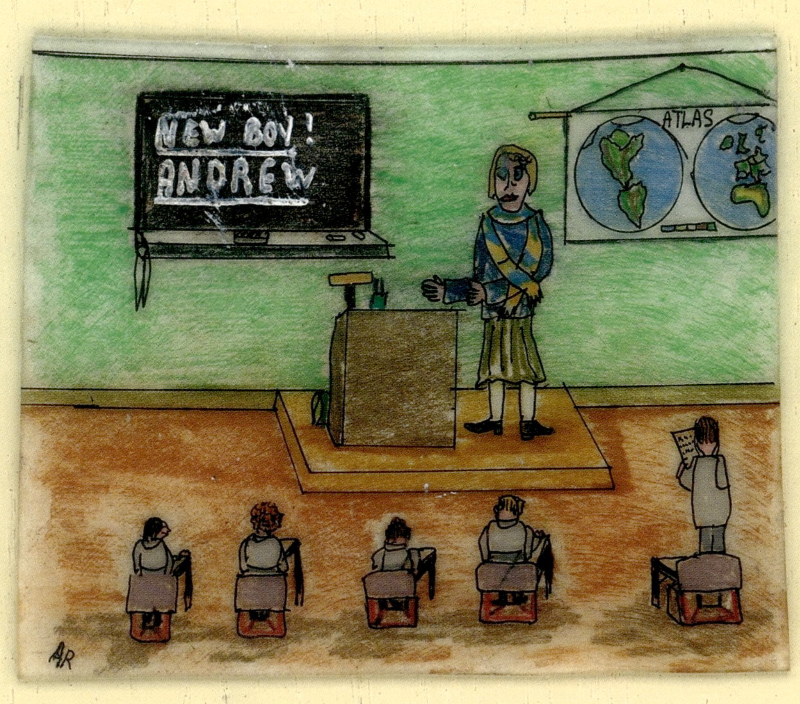

NEW BOY at SCHOOL

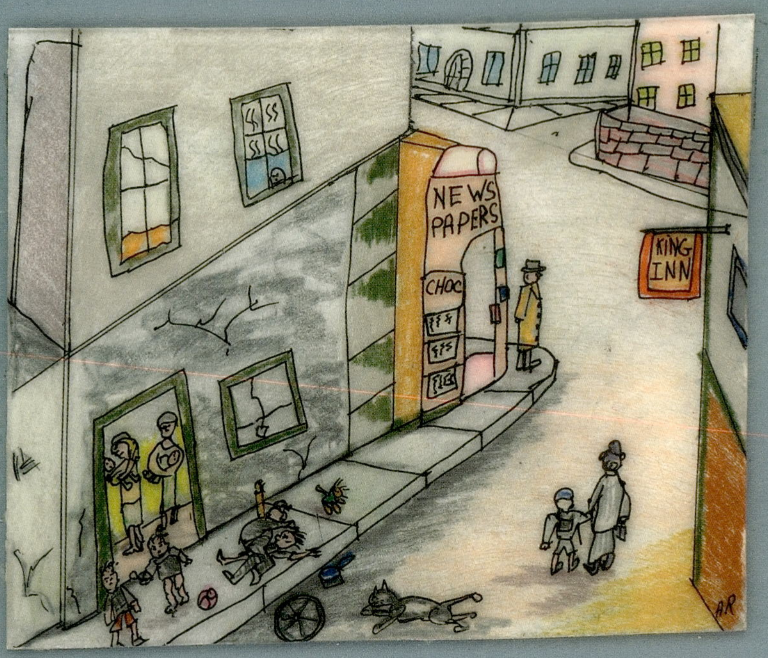

SIDE STREET OUTSIDE WINDSOR GREAT PARK

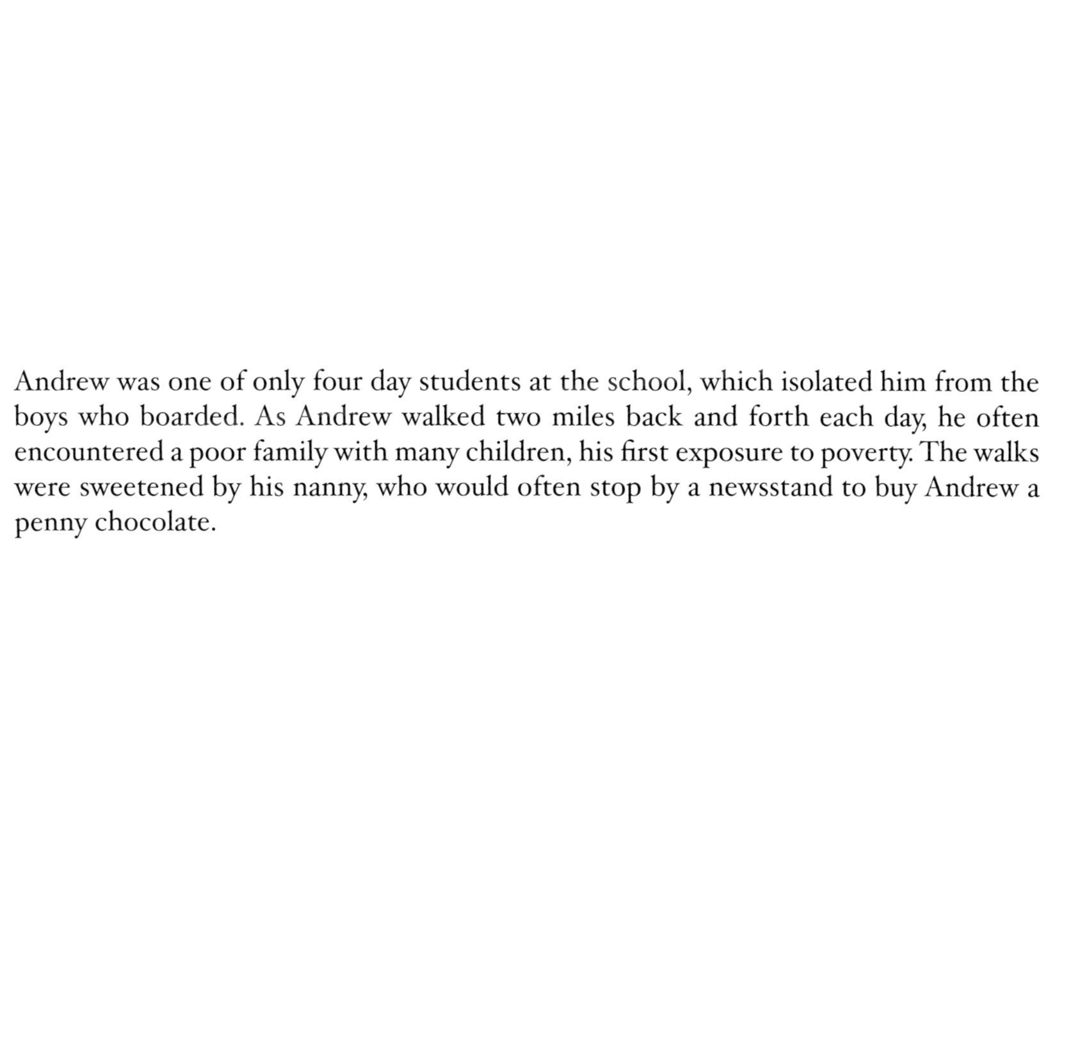

Andrew was one of only four day students at the school, which isolated him from the boys who boarded. As Andrew walked two miles back and forth each day, he often encountered a poor family with many children, his first exposure to poverty. The walks were sweetened by his nanny, who would often stop by a newsstand to buy Andrew a penny chocolate.

Being a military school, the Imperial Service College was rife with rules. The school leaders, or prefects, disciplined the disobedient in full view of the others in a mezzanine above the dining hall. One particular prefect, who merely wanted to brag that he had caned a prince, spied Andrew placing his hands in the outside pocket of his jacket, something only the senior boys were allowed to do. The prefect punished Andrew with four canings to his backside.

The housemaster of Andrew's dormitory was more forgiving. When he discovered that Andrew and his friends were sneaking out to a pub to drink and play darts, he didn't say a word. He later told Andrew that he knew but had figured the prince needed the lessons in regular English life. Lucky for Andrew—he could have been expelled.

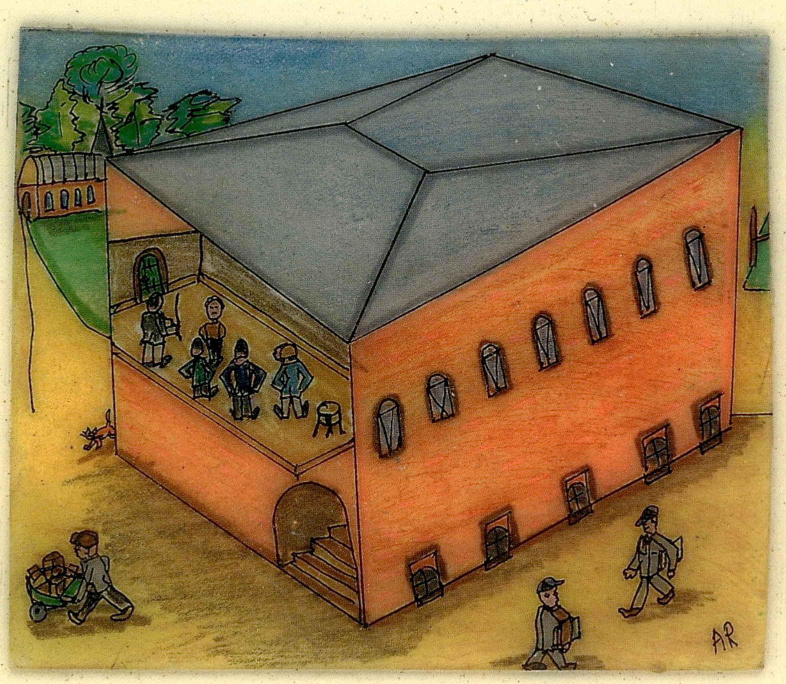

DINING HALL I.S.C. WINDSOR

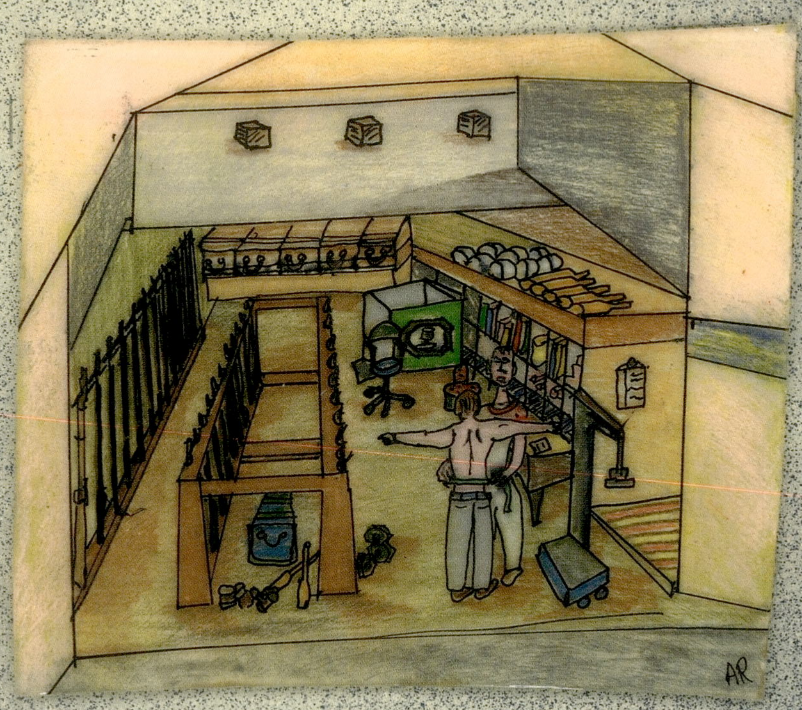

ARMORY CAPTAIN BARNES

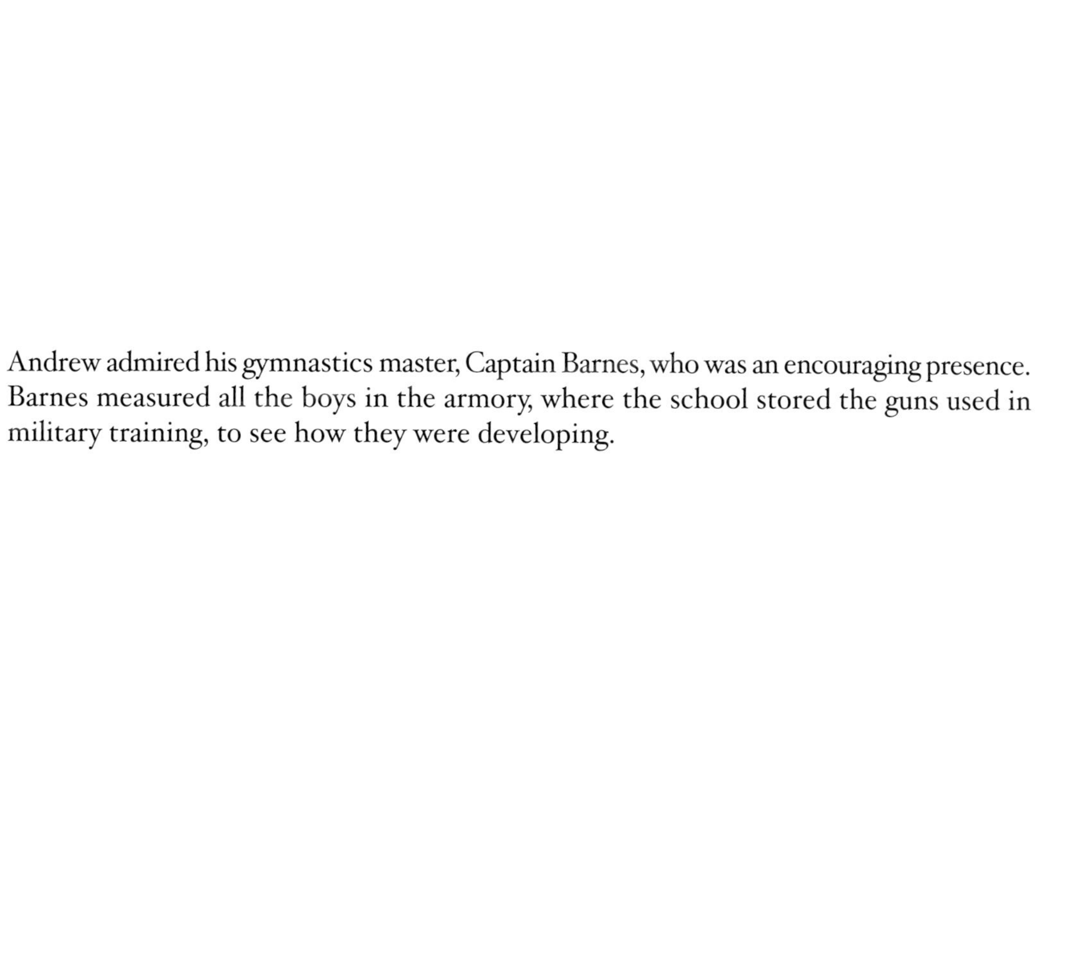

Andrew admired his gymnastics master, Captain Barnes, who was an encouraging presence. Barnes measured all the boys in the armory, where the school stored the guns used in military training, to see how they were developing.

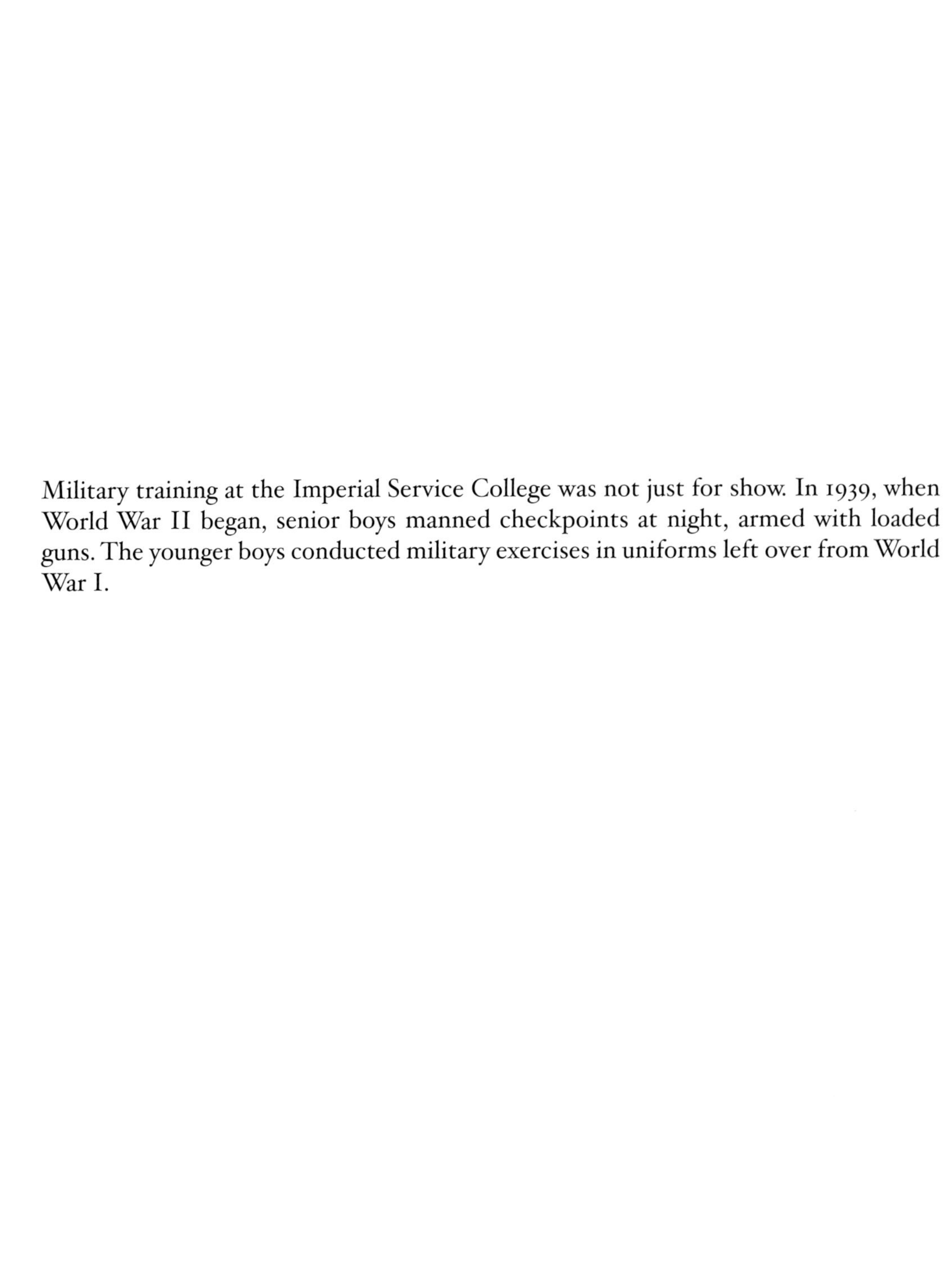

Military training at the Imperial Service College was not just for show. In 1939, when World War II began, senior boys manned checkpoints at night, armed with loaded guns. The younger boys conducted military exercises in uniforms left over from World War I.

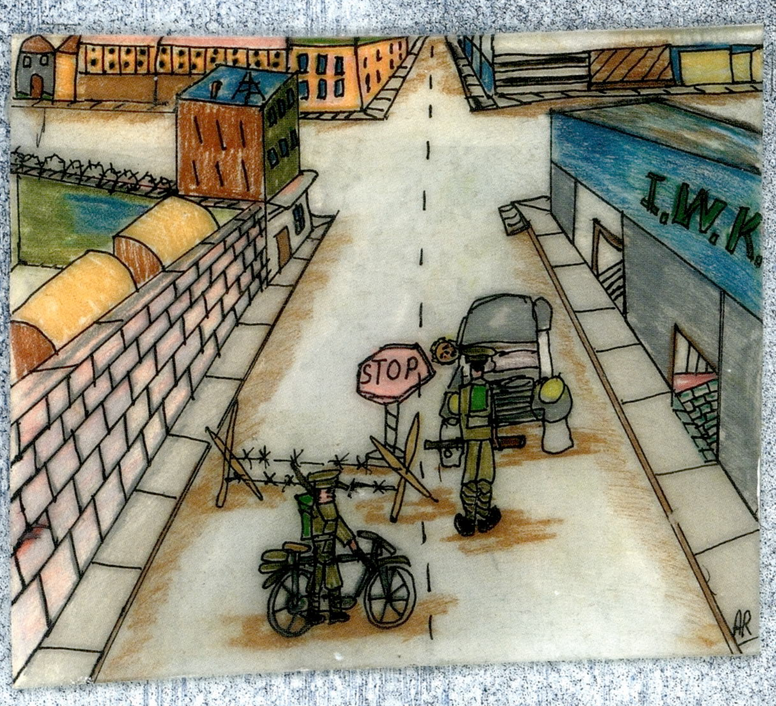

CHECKING DRIVERS for ID

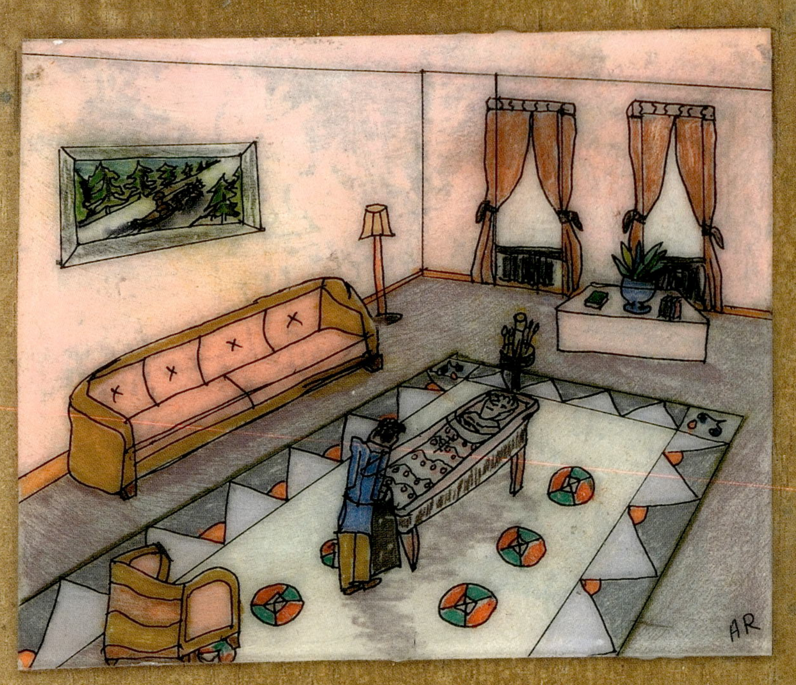

MY MOTHERS DEATH

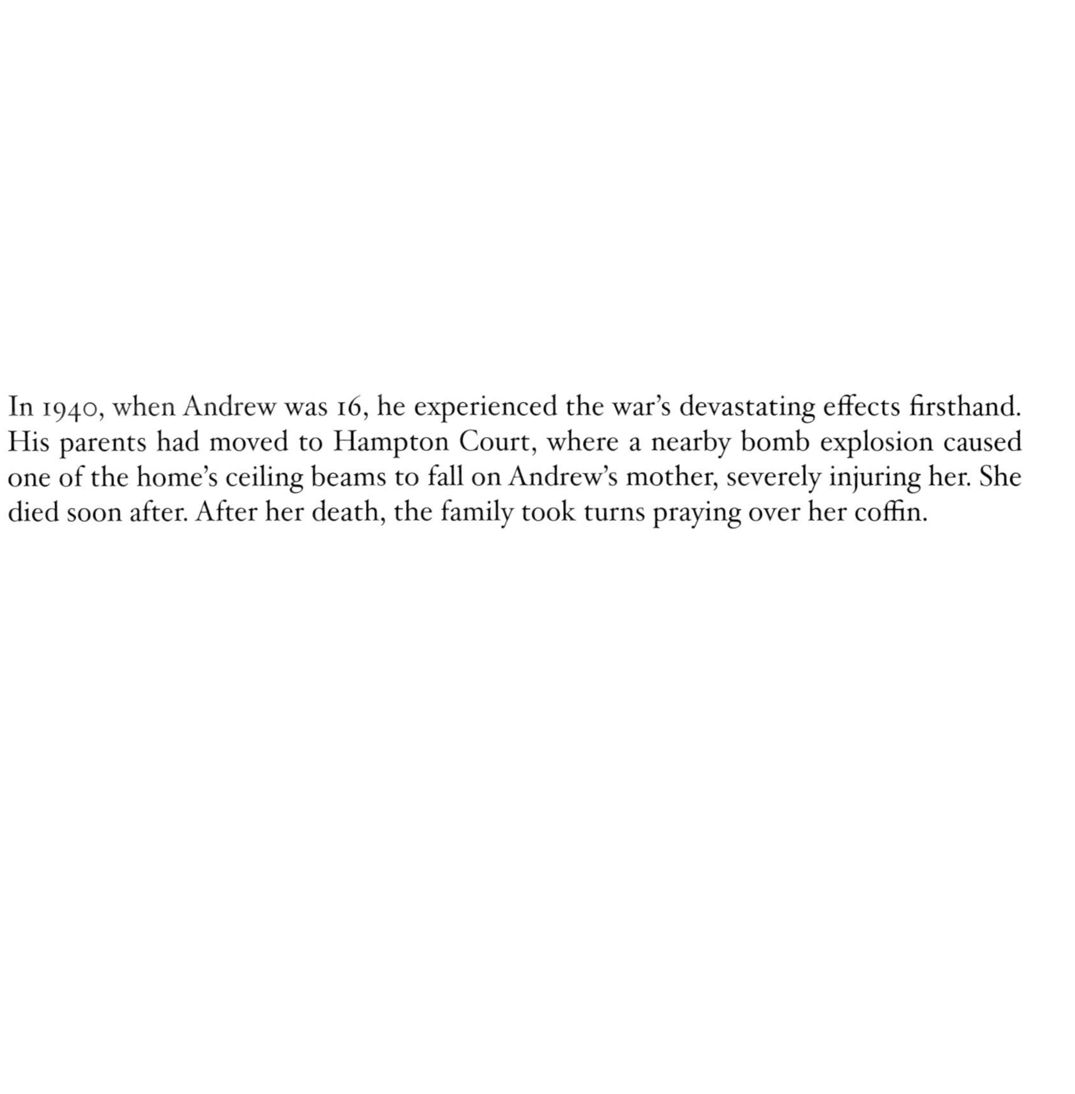

In 1940, when Andrew was 16, he experienced the war's devastating effects firsthand. His parents had moved to Hampton Court, where a nearby bomb explosion caused one of the home's ceiling beams to fall on Andrew's mother, severely injuring her. She died soon after. After her death, the family took turns praying over her coffin.

At the age of 18, Andrew joined the British Navy in the midst of World War II. But Andrew wasn't able to part with his youth entirely. Though his beloved stuffed kitty and teddy bear stayed at home, Andrew smuggled his stuffed koala, Winky, aboard his assigned ship in his duffel bag.

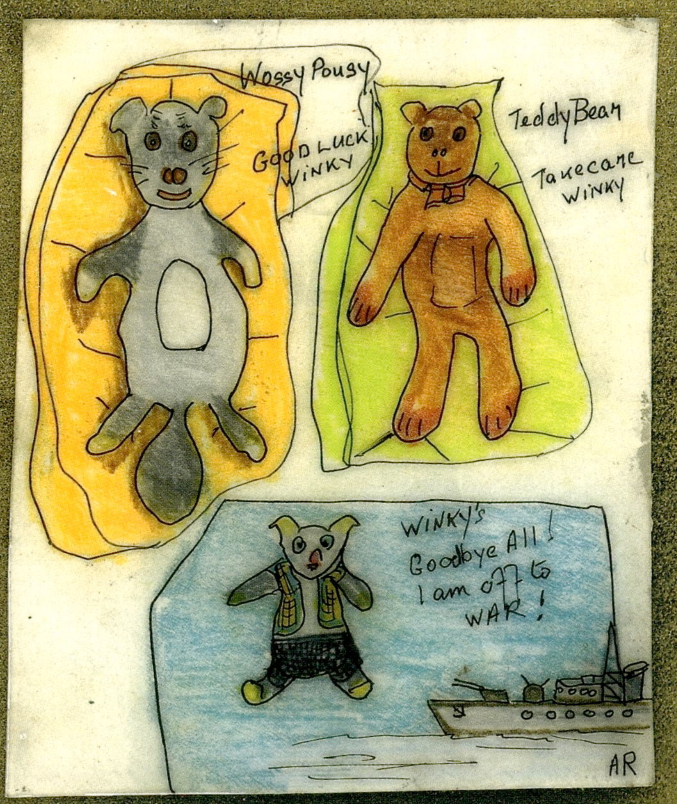

WINKY off to WAR TO H.M.S.NAVY
GOODBYE TEDDY and WOSSY-POUSY

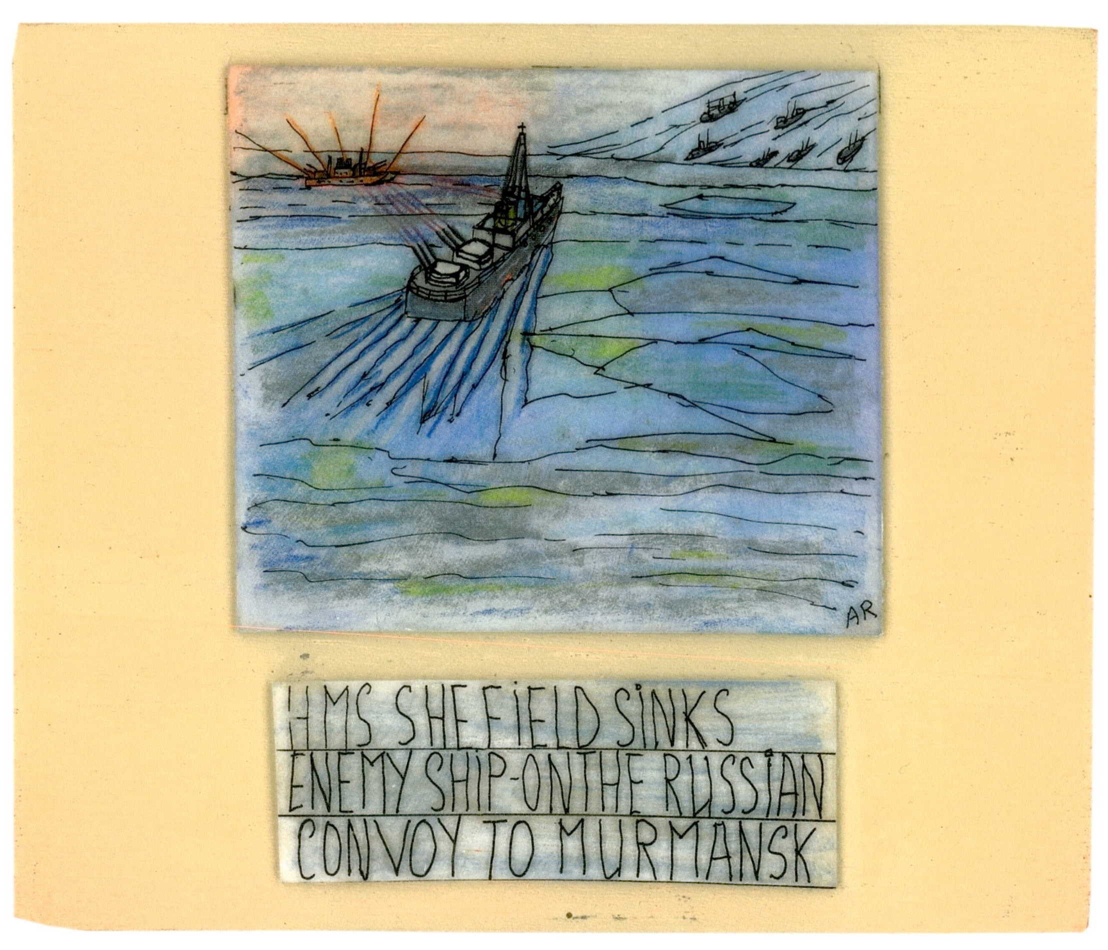

In 1942, Andrew was part of a dangerous mission in which his ship, the H.M.S. Sheffield, carried food and supplies to the Soviet people in Murmansk, a port in northern Russia near Finland. Cruising north of Norway, they spotted an enemy ship. The Sheffield signaled the ship in German, tricking the German ship into believing they were friendly. When the enemy ship came close, the Sheffield opened fire, sinking the boat.

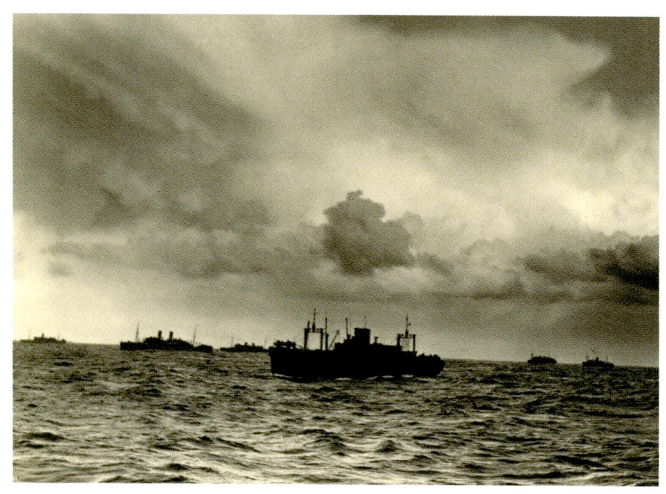

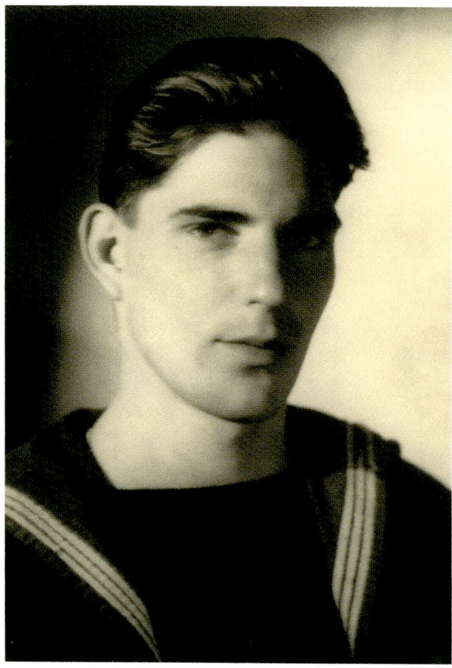

Andrew Romanoff, Royal Navy.

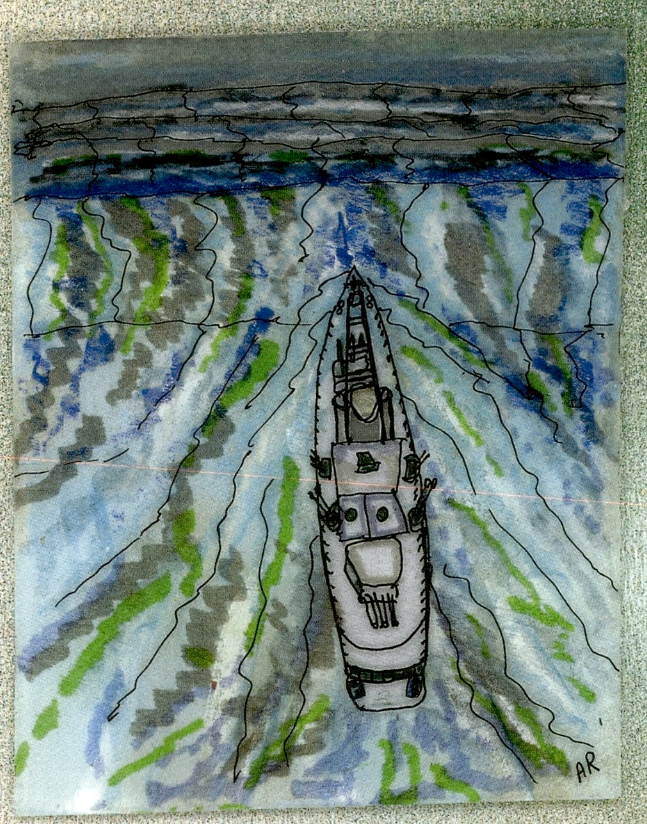

HMS SHEFFILD STORM 100' WAVES

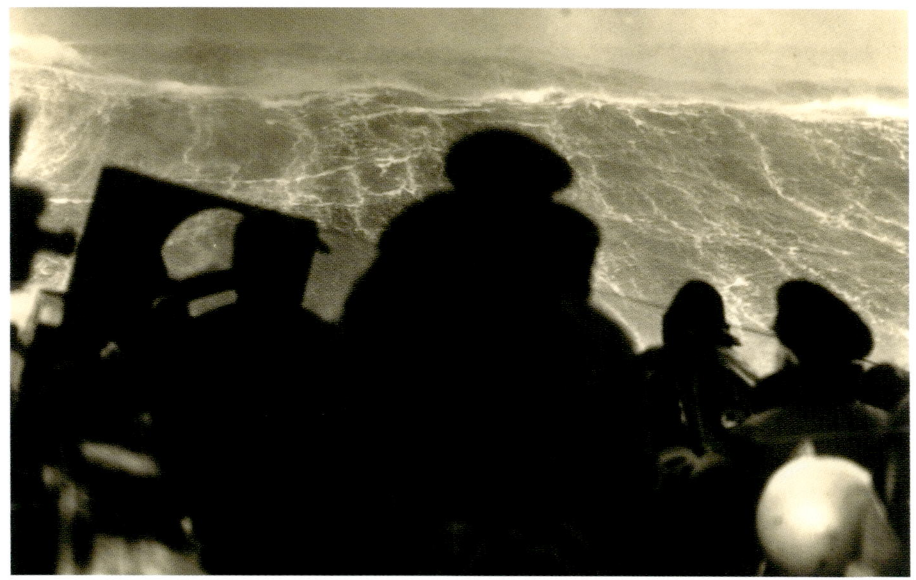

Photograph taken from the deck of the H.M.S. Sheffield.

Shortly afterwards, Andrew had another near-death experience. Cruising in the North Atlantic near Iceland, a storm arose with waves more than 100 feet high. The storm raged for more than 24 hours, while the chaplain prayed over the intercom. The storm, which sank four U.S. destroyers, was Andrew's most terrifying experience of the war.

While Andrew's royal status didn't exempt him from war, it allowed for a memorable experience while on break from duty. Andrew was visiting his grandmother in Scotland at Balmoral Castle, where she had moved to be away from the London bombings. A uniformed dispatch rider came to her house and invited Andrew and his sister Xenia to dinner that evening with the King and Queen of England at their Scottish castle. Andrew sat next to the king, who thanked him for fighting in the war. After dinner, when the group played a memory game, they were told that they must allow Princess Elizabeth to win, as it was her birthday.

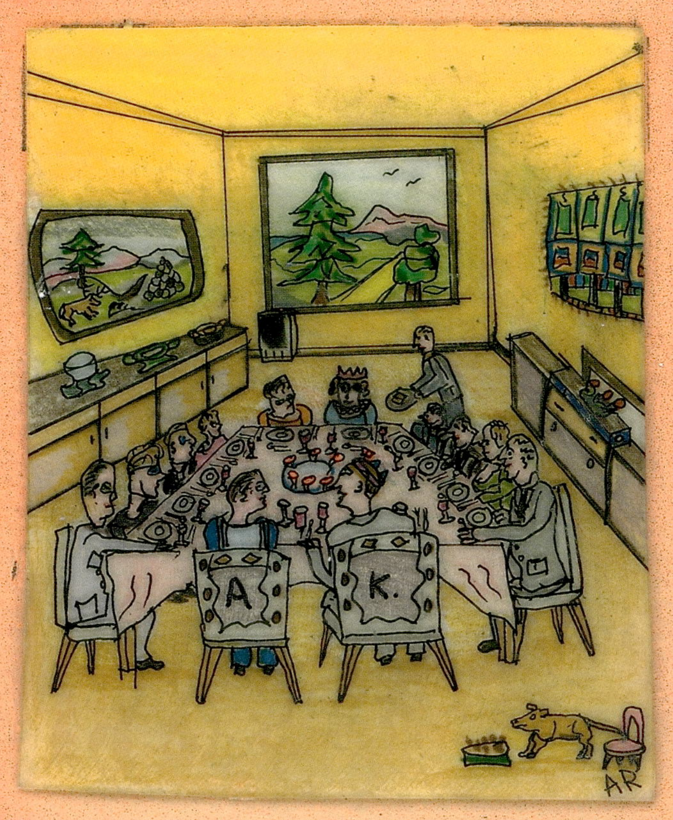

BALMORAL CASTLE
DINNER WITH THE KING AND QUEEN 1942

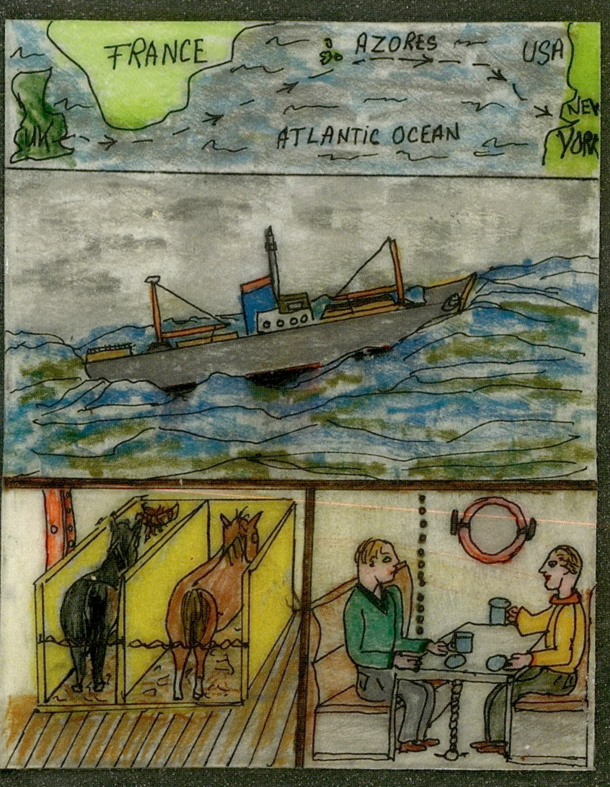

STORMY VOYAGE TO N.Y.
ON THE "AMERICAN MERCHANT" 1949

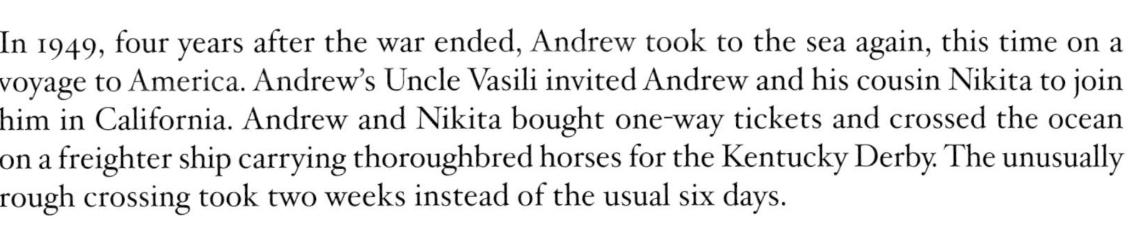

In 1949, four years after the war ended, Andrew took to the sea again, this time on a voyage to America. Andrew's Uncle Vasili invited Andrew and his cousin Nikita to join him in California. Andrew and Nikita bought one-way tickets and crossed the ocean on a freighter ship carrying thoroughbred horses for the Kentucky Derby. The unusually rough crossing took two weeks instead of the usual six days.

After their long, uncomfortable trip, Andrew and Nikita were thrilled to see the Statue of Liberty. After a week of seeing the sights in New York City, they took a Greyhound bus to San Francisco and met up with Aunt Natasha and Uncle Vasili.

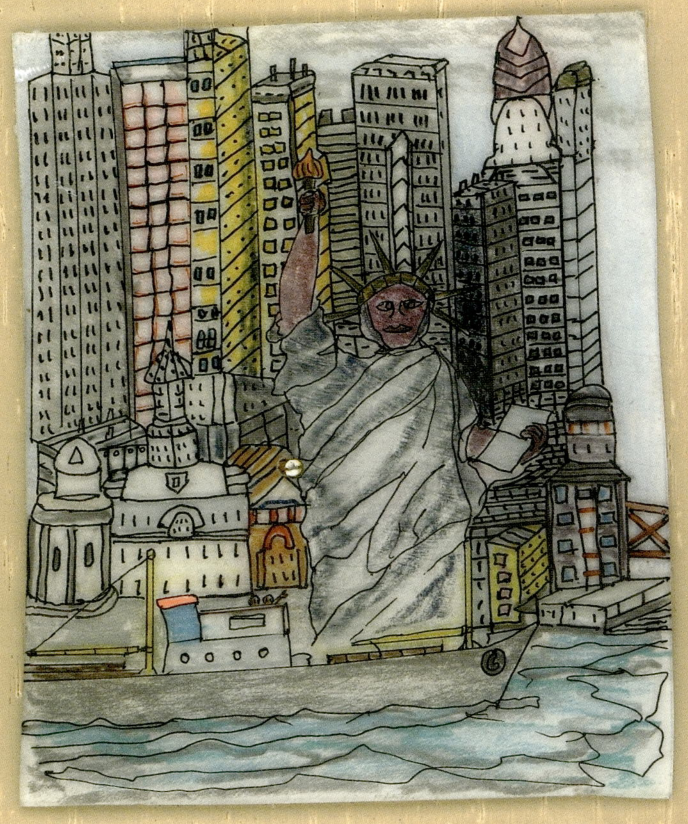

ARRIVAL IN N.Y. STATUE OF LIBERTY - WELCOMING

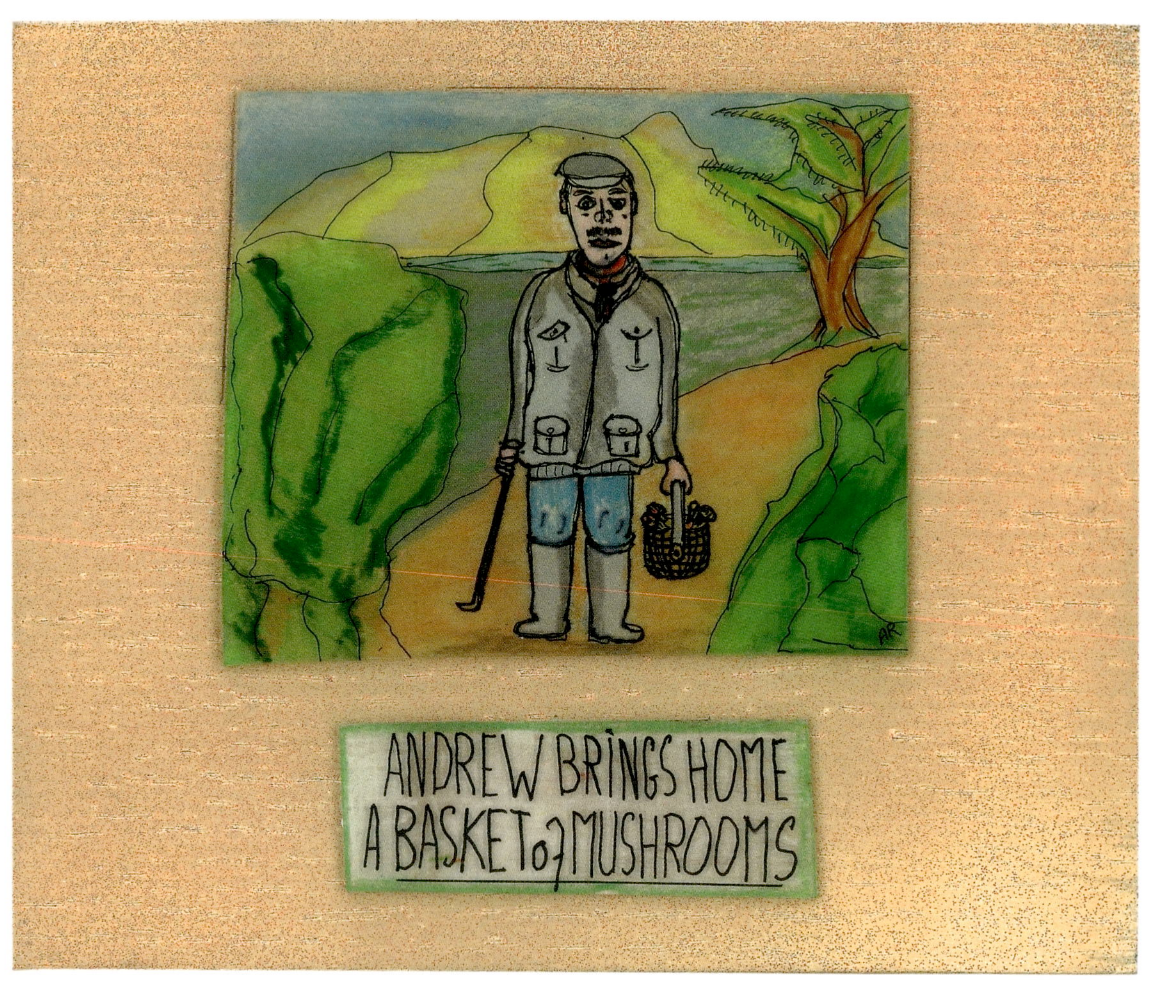

Now that Andrew was in America, he stopped using his official royal title: His Serene Highness Andrew Romanoff. Andrew, as he is simply known now, lives near San Francisco in a small town by the ocean.

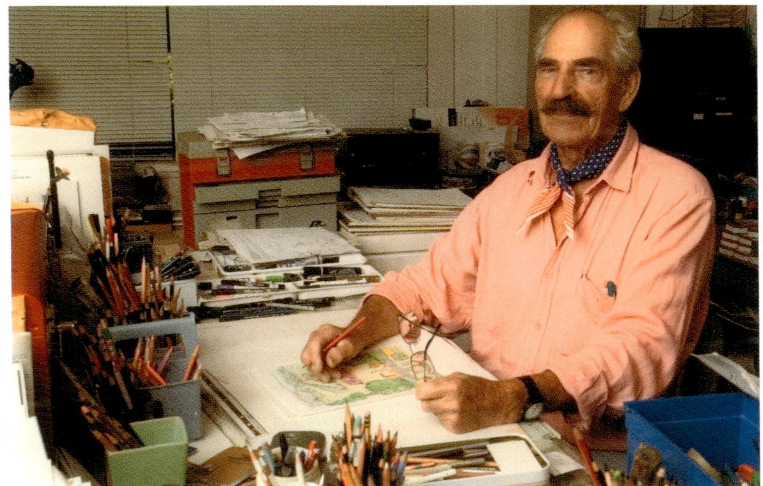

Andrew in his studio, 2002.

Charges to pay

______ s. ______ d.

RECEIVED

POST

TEL

Prefix. Time handed in. Office o

70

At ______ m

From ______

By

* TSA 99 12.25 LOND

PRINCE ANDREW ROMANOFF AM

DOCKS LONDON =

TAKE CARE OF YOURSELF

BON VOYAGE WILL FIND GO

LOVING PAPA AND NADINE

For free repetition of doubtful words telephon

at ... s should be acc

PAPA NADINE +

51-7098 MP